OSBORNE HOUSE
STABLE BLOCK
NOT ONLY FOR HORSES

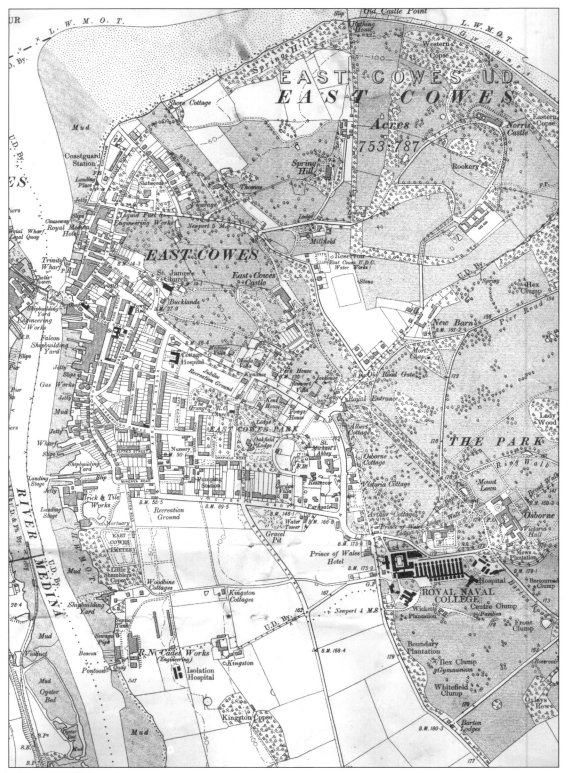

1909 map of East Cowes

OSBORNE HOUSE STABLE BLOCK
NOT ONLY FOR HORSES

The history of a nationally important building

By

Sarah and David Burdett

Foreword by
Michael Hunter
Art Curator, Osborne House

KSW
BOOKS

Cover illustrations:
Front - Original artwork: Newman Smith
Back - Original artwork: Tony Harrison

Printed by Crossprint
Isle of Wight
www.crossprint.co.uk

Contents

Introduction

The Osborne House built in 1846 at East Cowes on the Isle of Wight is best known as the private home of one family, a Royal family. Prince Albert helped to design the rebuilding of the old Osborne House as a peaceful retreat for Queen Victoria and their children.

In 1861 Prince Albert had new stables built in the grounds of Osborne House. The creation of this building provided a location for many different activities in the years after Queen Victoria's death.

In 2001 a planning application for changes at the 1861 Stable Block caused local historians to look more closely at the total history of that building. This book covers its various uses from 1861 until the early twenty first century.

Many aspects have been dealt with in detail in other publications. What this book does is to link them together and highlight the impact on the communities of East Cowes and Whippingham. This publication also shows why the community of this area should be proud of the achievements of former residents, both temporary and permanent, connected with this history.

Foreword

Queen Victoria spent a quarter of her long reign living on the Isle of Wight and Osborne, her family home, stands as a link to one of Britain's most fascinating monarchs. Queen Victoria and Prince Albert brought up a family of nine children and they spent some of their happiest days at Osborne.

After Queen Victoria died her rooms at Osborne were preserved and soon opened to the public. It is still possible to visit these rooms and experience them in much the same way as Victoria and Albert did. However parts of the house and many of the buildings on the Osborne estate that were designed to support the royal family's lifestyle were used for other purposes and as a result they remain comparatively unknown.

This book, devoted to one of these buildings - the Osborne stables - reveals the extraordinarily rich history of an important part of the Osborne estate. It is concerned not only with the role the stables played during Queen Victoria's time but with the building's subsequent story. The book spans two and a half centuries and using the stables as a spring board it clearly demonstrates how important Osborne continued to be even after it was no longer a royal residence.

Many discoveries have been made and I am sure this fascinating book will inspire yet more people to discover and enjoy Osborne, its buildings and estate, and the place they have in the history of the Isle of Wight and beyond.

Michael Hunter, MA (Hons) FRSA
Art Curator, Collections Department, Osborne House.

CHAPTER ONE

1784 – 1861
The Blachford Stables

This chapter contains background information. It is written to try to give some idea of the completely different life the owners of the Osborne estate led in the late 1700s due to the fact that horses were the main form of transport, other than walking, for everyone. Horses were valuable and the owners invested in their care. The equine industry became, by the 1800s, as large an industry as the automotive industry is today.

The land of the East Cowes peninsular is gravel overlying clay, not good farming soil. The Osborne estate, overlooking the Eastern Solent towards Portsmouth, changed hands several times without much investment being made. In the 1600s a dwelling had been built on the estate. In 1672 the owner, Elizabeth Mann, married Captain Robert Blachford of Fordingbridge in Hampshire. The Blachfords were a successful merchant family. Elizabeth and Robert had two sons. The younger, John, bought Bowcombe Manor on the Island south of Newport and became Lord Mayor of London in 1750. The elder son, Robert, lived at Osborne. His son, Bridges Blachford, named after his mother's family, became the church warden at St Mildred's, the church for the parish of Whippingham that included the Osborne estate, and Overseer of the Poor as well as a benefactor to the community. His son, Robert Pope Blachford, married Winifred Barrington of Swainstone Manor, also on the Island, and inherited Osborne in 1768. The family had prospered and, in 1774, Robert demolished the old house and spent a considerable amount building a large comfortable family home.

Robert employed an architect to draw up plans for a new house. The first action was to build a brick kiln and make moulds. Marl was brought over from Fareham and lime from Portsdown for mortar. The first construction in 1774

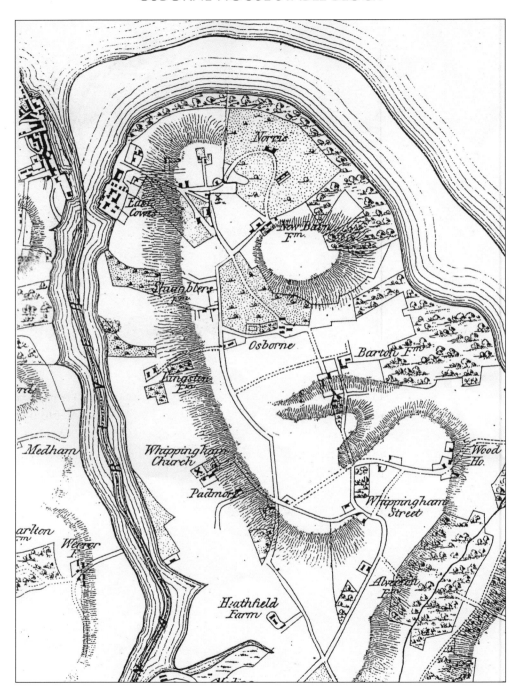

1800 map of East Cowes

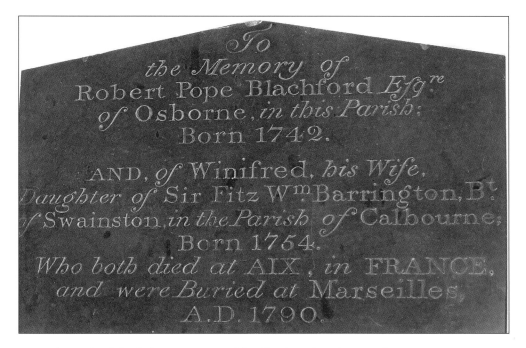

To
the Memory of
Robert Pope Blachford Esqre
of Osborne, in this Parish;
Born 1742.

AND, of Winifred, his Wife,
Daughter of Sir Fitz Wm Barrington, Bt.
of Swainston, in the Parish of Calbourne;
Born 1754.
Who both died at AIX, in FRANCE,
and were Buried at Marseilles,
A.D. 1790.

The Robert Blachford plaque in St. Mildred's Church, Whippingham

was the walled garden that remains in use to this day. A fifteen foot well was dug. Trees were imported from Holland. By 1778 a cart house and stable had been erected. The foundations for the house were then dug. Stone was brought from Chale on the south of the Island and smooth paving stones from Swanage. Westmoreland slate was shipped from Southampton. In addition to the bricklayers, stonemasons and carpenters, plumbers were also employed in the construction. The building was finally completed in 1782 at a total cost of £4,533. The house received praise in publications by local gentry and authors.

As a wealthy family the Blachfords could afford to care well for their animals. The stables consisted of brick built buildings with slate roofs. One side of the yard had a two stall and a four stall stable with a saddle and harness room at the end. The next side provided a carriage house for four carriages with a harness room at the end. A third side had a box stable, a three stall stable and a four stall stable and another stable for five horses without stalls. Above these there were three hay lofts and four bedrooms for men servants, each with a fireplace.

It may seem extravagant to have stabling for nineteen horses and this did not include the farm horses. The provision of various sets of stables was to cater

Osborne House as completed in 1782, the stable block to the left

for the different breeds required for different roles. One set of stables housed the riding horses with accommodation for the saddles and tack. The other housed the horses for the carriages with the carriage harness. The provision of different sized stables for the carriage horses may indicate that they were kept in teams for different carriages. Across the nation carriages were built to a variety of designs from a single seat Sulky to a large carriage to carry eight passengers; some were open and some enclosed. Each design had its own name.

Robert Pope Blachford did not enjoy good health and died in 1790 at the age of 48. Seven weeks later his wife also died. Their son, Barrington Pope Blachford, inherited the estate. His son, Fitzroy Blachford, was born in 1815. Barrington died in 1816. When Fitzroy died in 1840, his mother Isabelle Blachford was left with a large house and estate with no male heir to inherit it. The property was put up for auction in London in June 1843. To attract attention, it was pointed out that the adjoining Barton Manor estate with its 470-acre farm was owned by Winchester College who leased it out on a renewable seven-year lease. The advertisement for the freehold property of Osborne described it as consisting of 346 acres including New Barn Farm, and described the house as a substantial and commodious family mansion with excellent stabling. It did not sell.

Queen Victoria and Prince Albert, after some unhappy experiences, had decided that they must have a quiet retreat where they could live as an ordinary family. Victoria was familiar with the Island as she had spent two holidays as a

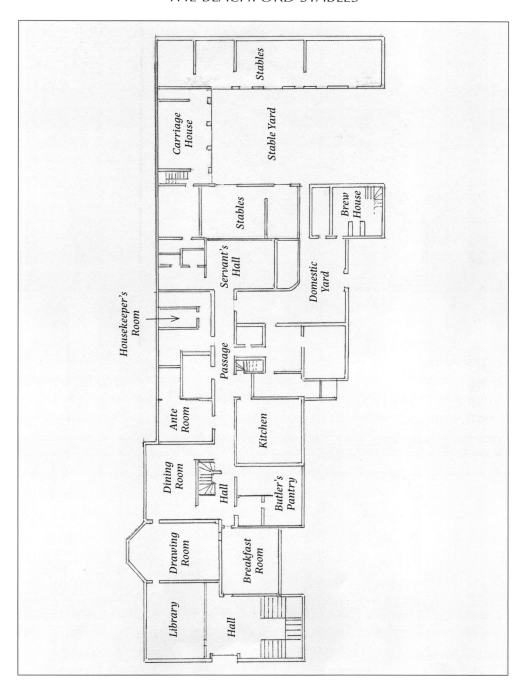

Plan of the 1782 Osborne House

Norris Castle, an engraving by Brannon dated 1831

teenager at Norris Castle, the adjacent estate to Osborne, overlooking the Solent. On her first visit in 1831 she had laid the foundation stone for the new St James' church in East Cowes. On her second visit, two years later, she had attended the consecration of the church. The Prime Minister was aware of the royal couple's wish to buy a property in East Cowes, so discrete enquiries were made. In October 1843 a letter was sent from Messrs Sewells of Newport to the Queen's Surveyor describing the Osborne estate in glowing terms. The price was quoted as £30,000 for both the Osborne Freehold and Barton Leasehold. Prince Albert wanted to know as much as possible about the property. He consulted maps and asked questions. The couple wanted to guarantee privacy, so Albert asked if there were any public rights-of-way across the estate, and was reassured that there were none.

Queen Victoria and Prince Albert were interested in purchasing the Osborne Estate but decided to rent it for a year in 1844 to decide whether it did, in fact, meet their needs. They only stayed there for a few weeks but it did confirm their wish to acquire the property. However they did also realise that the house would need some additions. After some negotiation, they purchased the estate for £28,000 in 1845. Albert immediately started making plans for a separate family

St James' church was designed by John Nash and completed in 1833

Osborne stable block of 1782, converted for domestic use in 1861. Photo 2019

NEW WING OF OSBORNE HOUSE, ISLE OF WIGHT.—(SEE PAGE 381

Old Osborne House and the new pavilion wing, engraving of 1846

wing. However he regarded the existing stables to be the best feature of the old house and retained the majority of those buildings. The Royal Couple employed Thomas Cubitt to draw up plans for a new wing for the family - The Pavilion. The foundations of this were dug by June 1845.

Lady Lyttelton, superintendent of the Queen's children, commented that in August 1846 the Queen dismissed many of the local workforce building Osborne so that they could take on harvest work. The men were told to return immediately they were no longer required at the end of harvest time and without fail they would again find work building at Osborne. Lady Lyttelton felt that this was doing good very wisely.

Victoria and Albert were able to move into the completed Pavilion in September 1846. The old Osborne House, apart from the stables, was demolished in 1847 to make way for the new Household wing in the same Italianate design as the Pavilion. The hay lofts of the old stables were converted to house some of the servants. All that remained of the old Osborne House was the front door, which was moved to make an impressive entrance into the walled gardens where it still can be seen today.

Prince Albert was very efficient in his activities and had a record kept of all the development and improvements that took place around the Osborne and Barton Estates and farms each year. These records were published in a book entitled *"The Works of Albert"*, a yearly record of developments at the Osborne and Barton estates and has a continuation list from 1861 completing the estate record to 1901. It is invaluable in dating many of the improvements carried out on and around the Osborne Estate. The book records that by 1849 the original Carriage House, with accommodation for only four carriages, was proving to be insufficient. So an additional carriage house was constructed next to the original stables complete with a stablemen's mess room. Water closets were added at the back of the stables.

Close to the original gate into the Osborne Estate was the coaching inn called the Prince of Wales. In 1854 Queen Victoria and Albert purchased the Prince of Wales Inn which became part of their estate. Here, when the Royal family were in residence at Osborne, servants of visiting dignitaries could be accommodated along with their mounts. Although the building of railways across the nation had commenced in the 1840s, the Island, with its small population, was slow to follow in this transport revolution. The first railway line on the Island, between Cowes and Newport, was not opened until 1864.

As time passed the global standing of Britain grew. So too did the standing of Queen Victoria among the European monarchy. Her own family was steadily increasing. The variety of functions that the new Osborne house had to meet increased, so that further expansion was necessary. In 1858 Victoria and Albert decided that a new separate stable block was required to make space for enlarged kitchens and additional servants' quarters at the house. Among the lessons learned over the centuries, especially on the large estates where best arrangements could be afforded, was that stables could be smelly places so it paid to build them separately from the main house and preferably down wind. At Osborne the decision was made to locate the stables nearer the main road, on the western boundary of the estate. Plans, which can be seen at the National Archives at Kew, were drawn up. The original stables that were absorbed into the royal Osborne House complex can still be seen today.

The design of an efficient stable is a specialist science. The buildings need to be well ventilated but not too cold nor too hot. The windows tend to be high up so that outside activity does not disturb the tranquillity of the stable. The grooming of a horse requires considerable water so, to avoid foot rot, stable yards need to be well drained. The flooring of the stable and the yard should allow easy cleaning because horses are not supplied with their own toilets. Having catered for their physical needs, horses need to be exercised so an exercise yard is frequently attached to a stable. To permit safe, comfortable travel the gravel roads needed to be regularly maintained, preferably with smaller stones that compact better and do not get stuck in horses' hooves. Along with the provision of good stabling went all the outside services required to allow the horses to do their work. These included the provision of feed, the making and fitting of shoes, the making of saddles and harness for riding and pulling carriages as well as the making of carriages. All these trades required for the Osborne stables had an impact on the Island community.

Osborne House was purchased as a private home for the royal couple. While the Stable Block had to cater for the needs of a Queen when in residence, the Royal couple had no intention of creating a grand stable block to match those of the wealthy estates. So the stables were designed to be efficient but in keeping with their family retreat. Thus was planned a building that was to have a very interesting history.

CHAPTER TWO

1861 – 1901
The Royal Stables

In 1858 Prince Albert inspected four sets of plans for new stables that had been produced by Thomas Cubitt and decided on one of them. Albert required an efficient functional building as needed for a busy family home on the Island, occupied for only part of the year. To this end Albert incorporated all the best stable design features in fashion at the time.

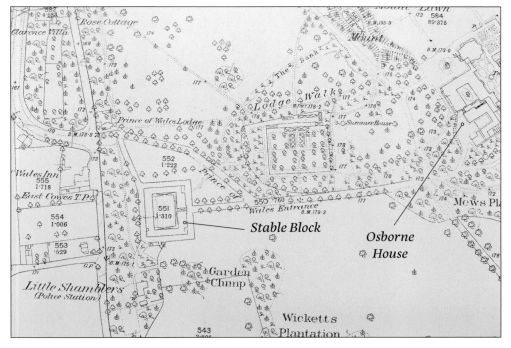

Ordnance Survey map of 1863 showing the new stables

The carriage entrance to the 1861 stable block.   Tony Harrison after a photo of 1875

It is interesting to note that by 1858 there was already a cricket ground at Osborne House, as, in December 1858, the Prince staked out: *"the ground for the New Stables which are to be begun by the back Lodge on the Cricket Ground, and also the new roads which are necessary."* This comment is from *"The Works of Albert"*.

Thomas Cubitt designed the stables and coach house around a central courtyard. In the same manner as the construction of the Osborne Pavilion, the stables were built of brick covered with stucco. This style had been used at Buckingham Palace by the architect John Nash whose home had been East Cowes Castle, only half a mile from Osborne. The main carriage entrance faced towards Osborne House. There were impressive doors in a three storey archway building. Inside the archway were the entrances to two sets of stables, each with stalls for 16 horses, giving a total capacity for 32 horses. As with Osborne House, the stables were built of brick from the Queen's brickyard on her estate located at the junction of Alverstone Road and Whippingham Road.

The stable floor was of bricks set on end, with proper drainage installed. These drains were extensive, with a three foot high drainage tunnel leading away from the stable block.

The divisions between the stalls were constructed out of wood with the same wooden cladding on the stalls' end walls. The marks of this cladding can still be seen in 2019.

One set of stables . Newman Smith after a photo of 1875

For illumination the stables had shallow windows under the eaves above the stalls on the external walls. A gas supply was laid to Osborne in 1860, a year after the East Cowes Gas Works were built in Clarence Road.

Albert proposed variations on the design of the stabling. He suggested open rafters rather than a closed ceiling in the stables. Mr Mann, the Clerk of Works at Osborne, suggested that this would cost an extra £50 on the estimate so a closed ceiling was built. This ceiling had vents in it leading to the louvered roof vents.

Stairs led up to the coachmen and grooms' accommodation in the

Stable cladding marks still showing in 2003

Archway view from the courtyard . Newman Smith after a photo of 1875

rooms above the archway. There were four small rooms, presumably for the senior staff. The main dormitory room was at the top with Venetian windows to the east and west, and was reached by a single staircase. It had cubicles constructed within it to accommodate eleven men. The room had circular windows looking to the north and south, one for each cubicle. Alterations post 1903 meant that these windows had to be blocked up, but their position was still apparent in the decayed paintwork in 2003 and recent redecoration has recorded their presence.

There were chimney flues on either side of the main archway block. These served two washrooms on the ground floor and two fireplaces in the grooms' room – there is space for them and part of the chimney breast is still visible. The Queen and Prince Albert provided good accommodation for their workers.

The archway led into a courtyard. Strong yellow bricks set end on in concrete were used for the archway floor. Red and black bricks were used for the wide patterned perimeter walkways around the inside of the courtyard. These are similar to those at Buckingham Palace stables. A glass portico

The courtyard walkway of bricks

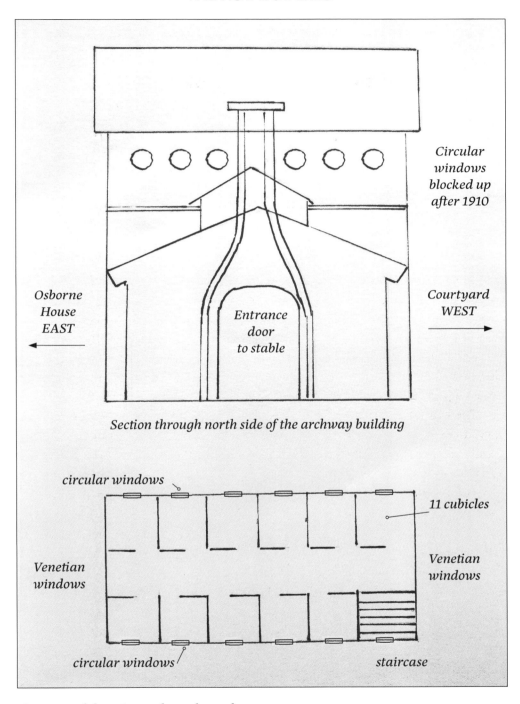

Section through north side of the archway building

The grooms' dormitory above the archway

was erected over the perimeter walkway. This walkway facilitated the preparation and grooming of horses, hitching rings being set in the walls at various heights for this purpose. A few of those rings remain in place. It is understood that Prince Phillip, Lord Louis Mountbatten of Burma and Lord Montague of Beaulieu each requested and were given one of the hitching rings during visits in the 1960s and 1970.

A hitching ring

Four options had been considered for the courtyard surface. Gravel would cost £120, broken granite £240, concrete and then 5 inches of Spanish Tar would have cost £640, and a concrete and brick faced yard £290. Albert opted for the cheapest option, gravel, probably because the family would only be in residence a few months a year and therefore a more hardwearing surface was unnecessary.

The archway originally fitted with two sets of doors

On the far side of the courtyard, opposite the archway, was a large carriage house with three entrances. There was a kitchen and dining room for the stable staff in the south west corner.

On the northern and southern sides of the courtyard there were harness and tack rooms. A cistern costing £108 was installed which could hold 22,730 litres (5,000 gallons) of water and a pipe bringing water to it from the Barton reservoir cost £137.

The carriage house and courtyard. Newman Smith after a 1875 photograph

The grooms' dining room and kitchen beyond

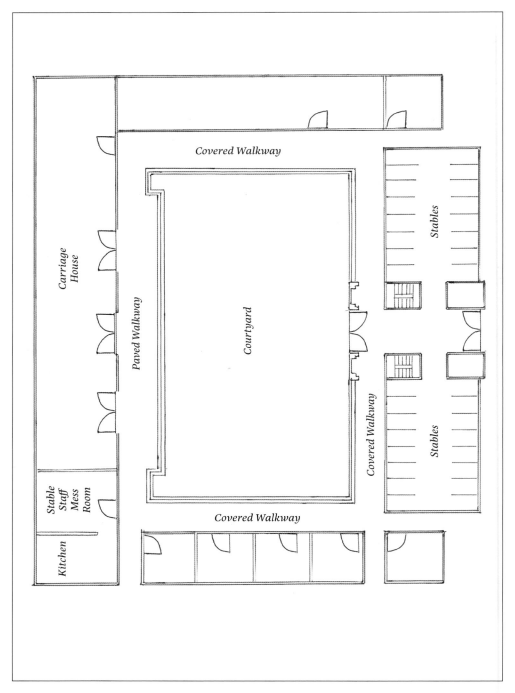

A plan of the stables before 1901.

The total estimate for building the new stables, as seen at the National Archives, was as follows:

Buildings and glass passage ....£ 7,800
Water supply from Barton ....£ 270
Barrel and outside drains .... £ 250
Yard gravelling ....£ 120
Total   £8,440

By December 1858: *"The stables had got on very much."* (WoA)

In 1859 a new road was made from the Prince of Wales Entrance to the new stables, and also from the archway to Osborne House. The alterations in the road system were felt to have succeeded very well. It was recorded that: *"a pretty addition has been made to the pleasure grounds."* (WoA)

In 1860 the new stables were nearly completed, with roads having been made all around the stables, fences erected and hedges planted. In January 1861 the new stables were occupied for the first time. The Osborne Stable Block was Prince Albert's last completed project that he saw at Osborne. He died on 14th December 1861 at Windsor.

In 1887 a telephone line was installed between Osborne House and Osborne Stable Block, nine years after Alexander Graham Bell demonstrated the system to the Queen at Osborne House.

The Staff

The Queen's staff moved around the country with her, with just a few people left behind at each of her houses to maintain the estate. The same happened at Osborne.

In 1861 the National Census was taken while the Royal family was in residence at Osborne – in fact the only time the Royal Visits coincided with such a census. Living at "Osborne Mews" were the following staff:

Coachman: 1 John Wagland
Postilions: 13   John Smith, William Head, George Bourner, William Riminton, William Maley, Robert Oakes, Henry Coestover, John Jones, Henry Hasswell, George Joiner, William Starke, George Legg, William Thorp.
Grooms: 9 Thomas Maldrett, George Andrews, Frederick Sayer, John Clark, Mark Thompson, Henry Baker, Charles Phillips, Henry George, Thomas Joiner.
Stable Helper: 1 Tolbain Gough

Postilions driving the Queen's carriages arriving at Whippingham Church

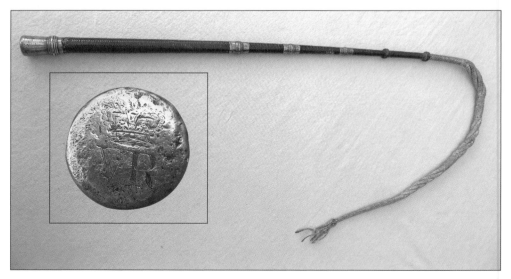

The whip engraved with VR belonging to George Bourner

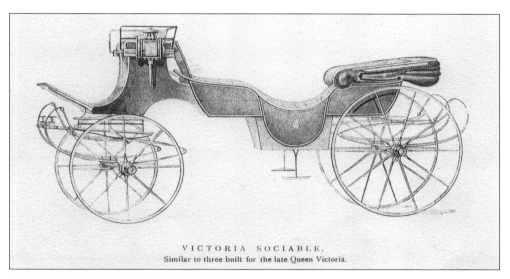

VICTORIA SOCIABLE.
Similar to three built for the late Queen Victoria.

The Queen in her Cheverton-built pony carriage

John Brown at the head of Queen Victoria's pony, Flora

carriages were made by the Chevertons for Queen Victoria over the years. The Chevertons also supplied sets of harness for the Royal carriage horses, made in blue or red patent leather.

Following the Queen's patronage, the firm of Cheverton received orders from all over Britain for carriages – providing the firm with an export business! The Queen also ordered other vehicles from the firm, as diverse as snow sleighs, barouches and bathing carriages, which were dispatched to other Royal Households on the continent. The Queen had a carriage called a sociable barouche built by Chevertons in 1880 as a present for her daughter Princess Louise. This carriage was used by Princess Louise until 1930 in London.

The most frequent route for the carriages was to the Trinity House Depot in the High Street in East Cowes to collect or deliver visitors, mail and despatches.

Horses

What do we know of the Queen's horses?

The royal horses and ponies would often accompany the family as they moved about the country. The children's riding tuition would continue at Osborne. From pictures of the family at Osborne, various horses were known to have been

Princess Beatrice on her pony Donald with Dacko

here. There is the famous picture by Landseer of Queen Victoria sitting on her pony *Flora*, reading her correspondence, with John Brown standing at the pony's head. There is also a painting of Princess Beatrice on her pony *Donald*.

In 1863 Mr W Megers was looking after the Queen's riding horses at the Osborne Stables. During the lifetime of HRH the Prince Consort there were ten horses from the Master-of-the- Horses Department for the use of Her Majesty the Queen and the Royal Family. Megers wrote, *"The Master of the Horses informed me last year that it was her Majesty's command to put 16 horses under my charge, namely 10 ladies horses and those 6 horses that had been used by my dear master..."*

He went on to list the horses he had; *Nimrod, Pompey, Violet* and *Edgar* (the old chargers) .....*Aja* and *Andress* which had been turned into ladies horses... Ladies Horses; *Alma, Ferodot, Thorheed, Samson, Dinhora, Classido,* and *Miles.* He also had a young filly now in hand to break for Her Majesty the Queen. *Alma, Aja* and the old Arab *Ferodot* were only to be used gently now, so he felt that he had insufficient mounts available for the Royal family at Osborne as two other horses had been returned to the mainland.

The Royal Yacht Victoria & Albert II at Trinity Wharf after 1896. (Dinnis Family)

Obviously it was a complex business having sufficient mounts for all the Royal Family to use when they were in attendance on the Queen. The driving horses were under the charge of another man. He had to have horses ready for the Queen to drive around the estate. If she wanted to visit the church, the vicarage or school, a carriage would be required. Carriages had to be ready to

The Queen drives through the new Trinity House entrance in 1845

stone in May 1856. This hospital was built in addition to the existing Royal Navy hospital at Haslar, near Gosport. Netley was the largest military hospital in the country and, at the time, was the longest building in the world. The building was 435 metres long and contained 1000 beds in 138 wards. In 1865 a cast iron pier 170 metres long was built out into the Solent to facilitate the landing of the injured from hospital ships. As the pier did not reach water that was deep enough, patients had to be transferred by small boat to the pier. Queen Victoria frequently visited the hospital, landing at the pier from the royal yacht. The Second Boer War of 1899 to 1902 again caused many casualties to be returned to England for treatment. Once the wounds had been treated the men needed to convalesce until fit for service again. In 1899 neither the War Office for the Army nor the Admiralty for the Navy had any provision for convalescing wounded officers and men.

In 1893 the brothers of Frank James had set up a memorial home for retired seafarers in 1893, in Adelaide Grove, East Cowes. In 1899 they provided pensions and found alternative accommodation for the occupants. They then changed the use of the building to a convalescent home for invalided soldiers from the South African War. The first patients were admitted on April 13th 1900. In 1902 the James Brothers offered the Home to Princess Beatrice with an endowment

Frank James Cottage Hospital, East Cowes

The household wing became a Convalescent Home for Officers

The nursing and domestic staff in the early days of the Convalescent Home

as a Cottage Hospital. The concern of the royal family for the care of wounded and sick military personnel probably brought this subject into the discussions about Osborne House. Due to its proximity to Netley and Haslar, Osborne House met all the requirements for the on-going treatment of injured officers. Hence the King Edward VII Convalescent Home for Army and Naval officers came into existence by an Act of Parliament in 1904. The building was put into the care of the Commissioners of Works.

In the Spring of 1904 the medical staff took up residence at Osborne House and accepted the first patients. The men were not fit for much in the way of active pastimes, mainly walking around the house and down to the beach or playing a gentle round of golf. This left the rest of the estate, without a particular function, being managed by the Commissioners of Works.

A Royal Naval College for officer cadets – sail makes way for steam

In 1900 the Admiralty had a major problem regarding the training of their officers and men. To understand the situation, it will help to consider some aspects of the history of training young men to become officers in the Royal Navy. During the 1800s the industrial revolution had transformed the Royal Navy from armed wooden sailing vessels, that had been developed as efficient fighting machines, into a fleet of iron hulls crammed with machinery and not a sail in sight.

In 1854 John Arbuthnot Fisher, later commonly known as Jackie Fisher, joined the Royal Navy as a cadet at the age of thirteen. At the time the Navy employed 5,000 executive officers commanding 55,000 men. In 1863, as a young lieutenant Fisher was posted to *HMS Warrior*, the most technically advanced naval ship of the time, as the gunnery officer. *HMS Warrior* was Britain's answer to the French *Gloire*, the first iron clad warship in the world. *Warrior* was powered by both sails and a propeller driven by a steam engine. The ship's complement consisted of 500 officers and seamen, 117 Royal Marines, two chief engineers, 10 engineers and 66 stokers and trimmers. The steam propulsion was mainly for manoeuvring in harbour. Her armament consisted of 68-pounder muzzle loading guns and 110-pounder breach loading guns.

By 1881, at the age of 39, Fisher was the captain of *HMS Inflexible*, the navy's latest and most powerful battleship. It was built with an iron hull 24 inches thick. It was powered by 8,400 horsepower engines that gave it a speed of 14.75 knots. Its armament included 4 x 16 inch guns weighing 80 tons, each muzzle

HMS Warrior

loaded by hydraulic machinery, and two bow mounted torpedo tubes. She carried 2 x 60-foot-long torpedo launches. She was equipped with electric light and separate tanks for water ballast to improve stability. *Inflexible* used all the latest technology *but still reflected the Executive's traditional approach – it was a fighting ship that also carried masts and sails.*

Fisher loved efficiency and the increased capability that modern technology provided. He did not subscribe to the philosophy of the traditionalists. By 1901 Fisher was Commander-in-Chief in the Mediterranean. At this time Lord Selbourne was the First Lord of the Admiralty, the civilian head of the Navy. He realised that the technical improvements in the Navy's ships had not been matched by the training of the crews that operated them. He knew that the training of young officers needed improvement. He appointed Admiral Fisher as Second Sea Lord, the senior officer in charge of the personnel of the Royal Navy, and gave him the job of implementing the Selbourne Scheme designed to revolutionise navy training.

This was only part of the situation when Fisher was promoted. In 1892 the Government adopted the policy of maintaining a Navy equivalent to that of the two strongest navies of the other European nations. Later in the 1890s the Germans adopted the same policy. The race was on. The political relationship between the European countries was slowly declining. There needed to be a rapid

HMS Inflexible

improvement in the quality of the fleet as well as the training of the crews that would man them.

During the previous century and a half, the training of teenagers entering the Royal Navy as officers had progressed slowly. In 1733 the Royal Navy built their first educational shore establishment for the training of young men intending to qualify as executive officers. This was the Academy built in the Portsmouth dockyard. It accommodated 50 young gentlemen who spent three years training to be Midshipmen. The alternative was three years aboard a man-of-war before they could qualify as a midshipman.

The Academy was augmented a hundred years later in the early 1830s by the 45-year old *HMS Excellent* as a gunnery establishment in Portsmouth Harbour. The Academy had a mixed history of success due to its location in the middle of a naval port. The environment was not the most salubrious. Portsmouth was a garrison town as well as a naval port with its associated social life. The sanitation was poor, and the air was foul.

In 1837 the Academy ceased to train young men prior to sea service. The building was adapted for the further training of commissioned officers. The training of midshipmen destined for the executive branch was carried out on ships in commission. In 1843 the Admiralty created the new title of Naval Cadet for youngsters training to become a midshipman. The formal training on board dedicated training ships moored in harbour resumed in 1854 with *HMS Illustrious* moored in Portsmouth to train young men from the age of thirteen. In 1861 *HMS Illustrious* was replaced by *HMS Britannia*. Two years later *Britannia* was moved to the quieter, healthier location in the River Dart above Dartmouth. By 1875 the Admiralty were again discussing whether it would be better to train cadets in shore establishments. A committee was set up to look at 32 possible sites. The education of these young men was still for them to be part of the Executive Branch with specialisation later for gunnery and other branches.

The Isle of Wight Observer of November 25th, 1876 refers to a possible new Royal Naval College.

"Portsmouth would like one but there are many drawbacks. It is not expected that the Isle of Wight will be selected to provide a site, but it is desirable to have a college near Portsmouth. It appears that the Admiralty Commissioners have been surveying an eligible spot near Fishbourne Creek at Wootton Bridge about one mile from Osborne. It is pretty and healthy with good facilities for boats and good access to Portsmouth. It would be good for the Island."

The Commission finally opted for Mount Boone Farm near Dartmouth as the best potential site. Despite this decision having been made in 1877, it was not until 1897 that the Admiralty declared that they would build a shore establishment for training naval cadets. Mount Boone Farm was purchased in 1898 but it was not until 1900 that the construction contract was awarded. The design of the college reflected the Admiralty's traditional thinking in training officers. There would be no engineering facilities at the college. The work was due to take three and a half years to complete. In 1902 King Edward VII laid the foundation stone of the main building.

Training of youngsters to become Naval engineers

Despite the comparatively rapid introduction of new technology into their ships, the Royal Navy had been equally slow in developing training programmes for youngsters as engineers. In the early days, those employed to look after the machinery were regarded in the same way as those who looked after horses – useful but of no great social standing. Commercial shipping had been the pioneers in the use of steam engines. So, when the Navy started to use steam

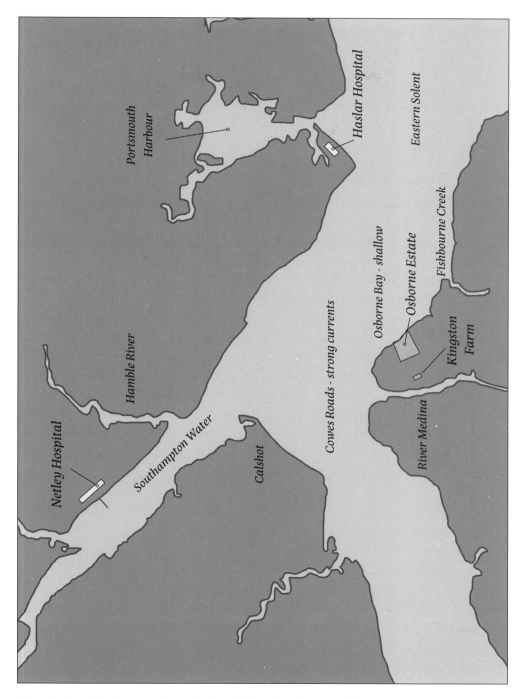

The relationship between hospitals and the Convalescent Home

engines, they employed men from the merchant marine. They were employed as civil servants not as naval personnel. By 1829 the Navy were giving youngsters five-year apprenticeships as Engineer's Boys aboard steamships. In 1836 Naval Instructors were introduced at Warrant rank.   In 1837 an Order in Council *established Royal Navy engineers as officers next below carpenters.* 1838 saw a training scheme established for Engineer's Boys (classed as apprentices) in the Navy Dockyard workshops at Portsmouth, spending two years in the Dockyard with one year between spent at sea. In 1843 proper schools were established within the Navy Dockyards at Woolwich, Sheerness, Portsmouth and Devonport for the training of both Dockyard Apprentices and Engineer's Boys.

In 1863 a more formal training was introduced for Engineer Students to replace the Boys' Training Programme. These started their training at fifteen. Education was extended to six years in the Naval Dockyards with two evenings a week at school to take account of the technical advances that were taking place. They wore naval uniform and were subject to naval discipline and entered the Navy after their final examination. At the same time the Royal Navy engineers began wearing purple stripes of rank. However, the engineers were still expected to mess separately from the other officers. In 1868 the rank of Engine Room Artificer was introduced in the navy. These men were employed to do more of the physical work of operation, maintenance and repair, in place of engineers. In 1873 Greenwich Royal Naval College was opened for the training of engineers, constructors and military officers, the Royal Marines. Each of these branches messed separately. When Navy ships visited foreign ports "to show the flag" the engineers were not considered to be of sufficient social standing to be invited to formal functions.

In 1875 the Cooper-Key committee investigated the most scientific and practical management of engines and the highest mechanical skill required for their maintenance for the Navy.
They recommended: -
Equality of pay, rank and promotion for engineers,
Abolition of separate engineers' messes,
Incorporation of engineers into the military branch, but not in command,
Greater scrutiny of Engineer Student candidates' social background,
Establishment of a residence for engineer students in the dockyards,
To train engineers to the discipline of a man-of-war.
The recommendations must have come as a shock to the traditional mind-set

The dining room in the old carriage house

block. The other rooms around the courtyard were given larger windows and eventually converted to nine more classrooms.

Despite all this work, there was still a lot to do as indicated in another article from the IoW County Press of the 5th of September '03 which reported that the Victoria Barracks in Albany Road, East Cowes, were to be used to temporarily accommodate a detachment of Bluejackets (Seamen) and Marines attached to the Royal Naval College. These men moved into their barracks and canteen at the College in 1904.

The Osborne Royal Naval College was declared open with little ceremony. After all, the Osborne Royal Naval College was initially intended to be only a temporary expedient until the Britannia College was completed. The first 72 Cadets took up residence at Osborne on the 15th September under the charge of a Captain, fourteen officers plus petty officers and instructors together with a Headmaster and nine academic staff. The facilities must have been fairly basic for the first term or two as the college was still a building site.

This is commented on by the Editor of the first college magazine published in December 1903.

*" **Hammer, hammer, hammer!** All day long, outside the masters' common room and outside the classrooms as well, the noise has driven a good many frantic this term. However it is an ill wind that blows no good, and we are comforted in our tribulation by knowing that this head splitting, heart breaking hammering means a new common room, new laboratories and new class rooms. New dormitories have*

The mast and the dormitories

A photograph taken from the mast by Cadet Lowry

been springing up fast and next term Osborne will hardly know itself for buildings." How the first cadets managed to study with all the building work going on is difficult to imagine.

The Admiralty paid Osborne House Convalescent Home £50 for damage done to the estate roads by the contractors during the construction of the college. East Cowes Urban District Council asked the Admiralty if they felt disposed to contribute towards the cost of repairs to the gravel highways, considering the greatly increased traffic which had been passing through the district in connection with construction of the Royal Naval College.

The planned expansion of the fleet with the proposed introduction of the Dreadnought battleships increased the number of Cadets required under the Selbourne scheme. By December it was decided that, instead of the cadets doing their four years of training at Britannia before passing out as Midshipmen, the cadets would serve two years at Osborne before moving on to Britannia for another two years. Keeping Osborne as a permanent college would double the available accommodation. From this period the new buildings at Osborne, apart from the next nine Uralite dormitories, were built of brick to give a greater life expectancy. In 1906 some of the cadets went over to Portsmouth to watch the King launch the new Dreadnought battleship, the most powerful battleship in the world at that time.

Plunge Pool

Term Lieutenant's cabin

Coat Room

Reading Room

A dormitory plan for 38 cadets

The Transformer House opposite the Prince of Wales Inn

A letter from the Admiralty to the Office of Works in December 1903 was asking for estimates for servants' quarters, lecture rooms, laboratories, masters' rooms, hospital and quarters for a resident nursing sister. The Admiralty asked for a quick response as the buildings were required for occupation on the 5th May 1904. A reply from the Office of Works dated 26th March 1904 declared that the laboratories, science and lecture rooms would be completed on time. It goes on to say that additional lecture rooms could be fitted into the St Vincent block, the old stable block, and that these would meet the teaching requirements until the midsummer vacation. They had not yet received the estimate for the electric lighting. Finally the letter says that, with the exception of the Laboratory which is in the course of erection, the new buildings would be of brick. The fact that, in March 1904, the Office of Works still had not received the estimate for electric lighting makes one wonder how everyone managed during the hours of darkness for the first three terms.

Initially the Admiralty intended using gas to supply the lighting for the college as a supply already existed from the stable period. The East Cowes Gas Works had been built in 1858 just as work commenced on building the Stable

The water towers and entrance to the toilet block

Block. However, the Isle of Wight Electric Light Company had a good reputation and, in March 1903, offered reasonable terms. In June 1903 the Company, based at Newport, were contracted to supply electrical lighting to the college buildings on the estate and at Arthur Cottage, next to the Prince of Wales entrance, which was also used by the College. A transformer house for this supply still exists by the bus stop opposite Osborne garage. The transformer was required because the existing installation used a 105 volt supply, while the Company supplied

The large Toilet block built in 1903

electricity using the maximum voltage allowed by the Board of Trade of 240 volts. Two 150 amp meters were installed for the college. A 10amp meter was installed at Captain Wemyss's house on the college grounds and at Captain Powell's house. A 5 amp supply was installed to Park House and Olinda Villa, houses in York Avenue, also bought by the Admiralty for the College staff accommodation.

A water supply already existed to Osborne House and the supply was improved for the use of the college by the construction of a water tower next to the Stable Block. Each dormitory had a plunge pool incorporated at the north end. When the college opened, until the 4-inch mains supply piping was installed, water was initially supplied from Osborne House. A hot water system for the college was installed for £800, but this did not extend to the dormitory plunge pools!

A large toilet block was constructed next to the water tower. Sewerage disposal for the dramatic enlargement of the population of the Osborne Estate with its Naval College and Convalescent Home was provided for by building new drains and a modern sewage treatment plant in the estate woods near Osborne Bay. This replaced the septic tank system installed under Prince Albert's direction in 1845.

Another letter in 1904 to Mr Hawkes, the architect, says that the dimensions of the hospital wards, the men's dormitories and Petty Officers cubicles seemed somewhat excessive and should be brought down somewhat. There was obviously discussion about providing a church as the letter goes on to tell the architect that there should be no turret on the church plan and the door should be of Tudor character! This comment shows that the idea of an architectural theme was in the mind of the Admiralty as there is Tudor styling on the water towers that were built for the college the second being completed in 1910. A church was not built initially as the gymnasium block, Nelson, was used for that on Sundays and the Roman Catholic cadets attended services in the corrugated iron church that served the East Cowes Catholic community.

The college magazine *"Osborne"* for the Easter term 1904 notes that *"The great event this term has been the visit of His Majesty King Edward VII to the College on Saturday, February the 12th. He was looking very well. He visited Kingston, and the College buildings, Dormitories, "Nelson", " St Vincent", Class rooms, etc., and took a great interest in , and seemed thoroughly pleased with, everything he saw."*

The building of dormitories continued to accommodate the additional intake at the start of each successive term until the two year intake was completed. A total of twelve dormitories were constructed, the first three for 30 cadets each, the other nine were for 36 cadets. This provided accommodation for 414 cadets.

Nelson Hall and the chapel, with the Cochrane block and the stable block behind

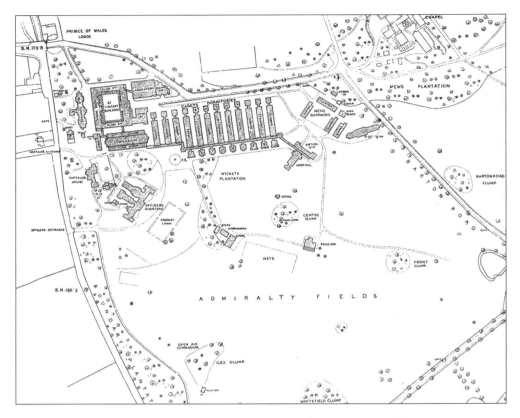

1908 map showing the covered ways connecting all the college buildings

All the dormitories were connected by a covered passage leading to the main buildings. This passage easily became congested. On the north side of this passage there was access to a coat room, a cabin for a petty officer and the entrance to the dormitory. At the foot of each bed was the sea chest containing all the cadet's possessions. There was a window for each bed space. In the centre was a solid fuel stove during the winter. At the far end was a door leading to the bathroom which contained a plunge pool four feet deep and ten feet square plus baths, hand basins and toilets. On the south side of the long connecting passage each dormitory had a reading room containing lockers for the cadets' books. The dormitory was the cadets' "home" from where he went to other parts of the "Ship" for his lessons, training, meals, and recreation.

As with most projects, the budget caused concern. In June 1904 letters were being exchanged about modifying the designs of some of the new buildings. The golf pavilion needed £600 spent on it. Several items such as the Racquet and

The linking corridor and reading rooms

Fives courts were not built. A small Chapel was not built until 1907. The Petty Officers and servants quarters were costing additional money. A London firm of Messrs W H Lascelles had put in the lowest tender and won the contract.

One of the plunge pools at the end of each dormitory

The Cochrane classroom block photographed 2018

In the specifications regarding the buildings put up by Lascelles, it says that the red bricks would be supplied by the Bursledon Company, based at Bursledon on the Hamble River. This would indicate that the Island brick yards could not supply the quantity required or at the right price. The tiles were to be *"Bromley tiles supplied by a reputable firm"*.

Additional classrooms were provided in the new Cochrane building that we can still see today, opposite the science laboratory. These buildings were built on each side of the road into the Stable Block archway. Next to the science lab, a building was constructed for the Headmaster's office and teachers' common room. At the eastern end of the dormitories a 14 bed hospital with two isolation bedrooms was built of brick, and finished in the summer term, 1905. Near the hospital, accommodation for the Petty Officers' Quarters was also brick built. It is now in use by English Heritage as a facility for visitors to Osborne House. The Captain's House was built to the south west of the old stable block. Servants' quarters were built between St Vincent and the main road. This must have been a large building because, when the college was fully operational, there were a total of one hundred catering staff and servants, fourteen for the officers and eighty six for the cadets. These were all naval ratings and, in the spirit of shipboard life, could be housed in dormitories.

The Head's office and teachers' common room on the right

In 1907 a recreation room for the cadets was built to the south of the four middle dormitories and eight squash racquet courts created between the cricket pavilion and the officers' mess. Later another gymnasium was built to the west of the Petty Officers' quarters.

Each of the buildings was given the name of a famous naval officer. The dormitory names were, starting at the stable block end and progressing eastward: - Hawke, Rodney, Anson, Drake, Duncan, Howe, Cornwallis, Collingwood, Blake,

The Naval Petty Officer Instructor's quarters

The Cadets' Recreation Room

Benbow, Granville and Exmouth. The large gymnasium was called Nelson. The Stable Block was called St. Vincent. The classroom Block was called Cochrane. In about 1909 the name St Vincent was changed to Collingwood.

In the summer of 1910 two libraries were built above the old stables, requiring metal pole supports to be located in the old stable classrooms. This extension provided two very large rooms upstairs, with large windows and roof lights. Each year had their own library and the signs to *"Library, 1st year Cadets"* and *"Library 2nd year Cadets"* still exist. The floors were of strong parquet wood blocks. The former grooms' bedroom above the arch was also treated to parquet flooring with a large stage or dais. Could this room have been used for dramatics or music lessons? We know that violin lessons were given to King Edward's sons when they were cadets at the college, and their violin tutor was transferred to Britannia with Prince Albert.

Sign to the Second Year Cadets' Library

One of the two libraries built over the old stables

Eight classrooms on the ground floor with two libraries above

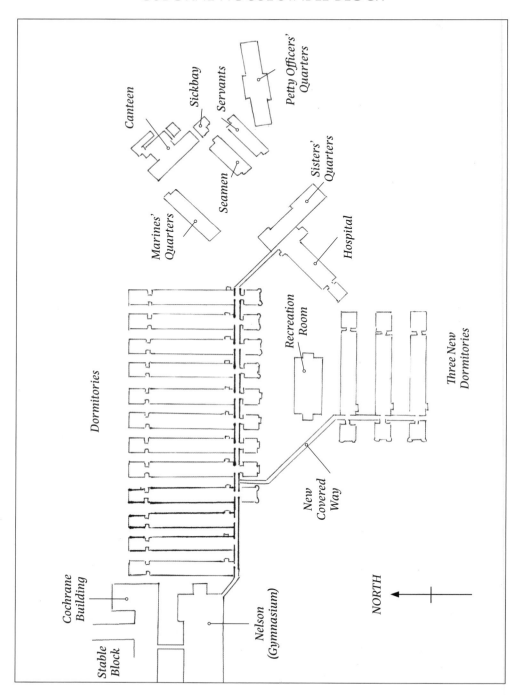

Plan of the college site in 1915

In preparation for possible conflict, three more dormitories were added in 1914, each for 38 cadets, to the south of the existing dormitories. This increased the total capacity at any one time to 528 cadets. By October 1914 the college had been enlarged at a cost of £102,000. There is a list of the number of cadets entering the college each term. This shows that the maximum intake was in 1915 when 336 cadets started their training. The total number of cadets at the college that year, including those starting their second year, was 549. The following year's entry of 313 would have made the total under instruction in 1916 of 649 if some of those completing their first year had not been sent to sea. Selbourne's foresight and Fisher's industry had ensured that the Royal Navy had the capacity to meet the demands of war.

The Engineering workshops

The establishment of the buildings on the Osborne estate, comparable to a moderate sized boarding school, was easy and simple. The major difference that made Osborne Naval College unlike any other used to train Royal Navy cadets was the construction of a set of brick built workshops on what had been Queen Victoria's land of Kingston Farm, down by the bank of the River Medina. These enabled practical instruction to be given to all the cadets in all matters to do with ship construction and engineering. These buildings cost £33,000. The Newport electricity company were hoping to make good business supplying power to what was in effect a small factory. However Admiral Fisher's aim for efficiency made the development team choose to have their own steam powered generating plant built at the workshops. In June 1903 the British Westinghouse company were awarded the contract to build the power plant for the workshops.

The workshops had a boiler house with a 90-foot tall chimney as well as a dynamo room containing two dynamos. The first workshop was aligned north/south and was fitted with three ridged roof-lit sections. It housed numerous belt-driven machines such as lathes and drills.

The engineering workshops

There was a laboratory built east/west with two ridged roof-lit sections. This became a lecture room and drawing office with a sun printing room off it. This, the smallest block of the workshop buildings remains, now within the grounds of East Cowes Power Station in 2019.

The remaining three lecture rooms in 2018

There was a carpentry workshop and a chemistry laboratory. There were offices for a Commander (Engineering) and a second office where, in 1903 Engineer Lieutenant H. W. Metcalf appears to be signing changes to the plans for the constructors. In 1905 a new smithy was added to the complex. The basic engineering instruction in the workshops could be easily followed up by experience afloat on the training vessel. The location chosen for the workshops could well have been influenced by the intention to provide the college with its own training vessel moored in the river.

The Cadets marched or "doubled" down to the works from the college, and a special path was laid for them, edged in heavy black "engineering" bricks. This pathway was named Cadets Walk in 1910 and is still known as such in 2019.

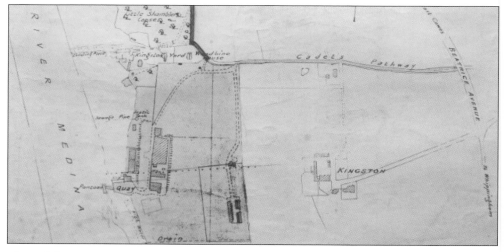

Plan of the site showing the pathway now known as Cadets Walk

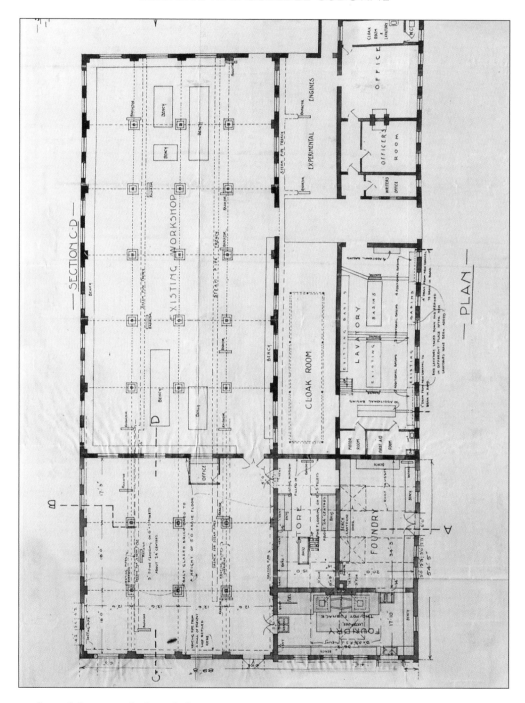

A plan of the extended workshops in 1912

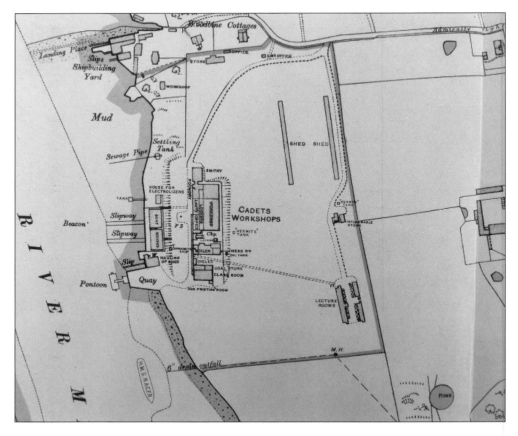

1910 map showing the location of the workshops

The Cadets would look smart as they ran down hill in fours accompanied by a Petty Officer, but were usually rather messier on their return journey from the engineering works.

The omission of engineering facilities from the design of the Britannia College meant that the engineering works at Osborne had to be used to the maximum advantage before the cadets moved on to Britannia at Dartmouth. This explains why the cadets spent half of every study day down at the Kingston Works by the river. Their instruction in navigation, which is an example of applied mathematics, was left until the cadets had furthered their basic education at Osborne and moved on to Britannia. All the cadets must have had a vivid image of Cadets Walk in their minds by the time they left Osborne.

The total cost of building the College including the Kingston Works, to cater for 414 cadets, was £159,804.

An aerial view c 1920, showing the 1915 extensions with lighter colour roofs

of the college there were instances of a high number of cadets being ill at the same time. Initially Park House in York Avenue was the sick bay.

An eight bed isolation hospital was constructed in 1904 to the south east of the Kingston workshops. This proved to be insufficient. In the summer term of 1905 a general hospital with sixteen beds was completed within the college grounds adjacent to the dormitories. This also had accommodation for Nursing Sisters. The covered way linking the dormitories was extended to the hospital. In the Easter edition of the college magazine in 1908 there is a report of a series of illnesses of 'flu, measles, German measles, mumps and scarlet fever. The patients were filling the sick bay, Park House, the wards at Kingston, the recreation room and the band room. The illnesses caused the college to close five days early.

Later, in 1908, additional Crown Land opposite the entrance to the Barton Estate was obtained where, by 1910, four hospital blocks had been built with accommodation for medical staff. The completion of the hospital was just in time. In 1910 there was an influenza epidemic at the college with 150 patients in the hospital at one time. The Barton hospital buildings were demolished in the late 1990s to make room for industrial development.

A medical report on the college commented that the water in the plunge pools should be changed more frequently. The local authorities asked the Isle of

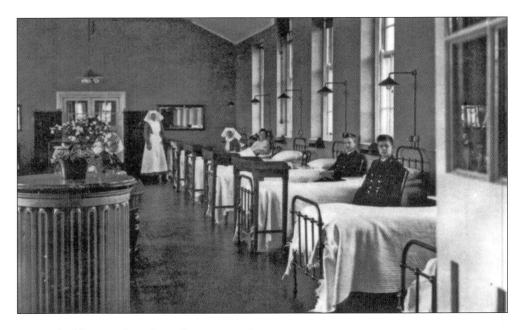

The 12 bed hospital on the college grounds

The hospital opposite Barton Manor, in use by Saunders Roe c1960, with long test tanks on the right

Wight Rural District Council (IWRDC) staff at Carisbrooke to test the quality of the water supply. The supply to Osborne was found to be excellent. It was agreed that the IWRDC would supply the college with a minimum of 6,000 gallons a day at a cost of one shilling and nine pence per 1,000 gallons. East Cowes Urban District Council could only supply 2,000 to 3,000 gallons per day. In 1913, despite taking special precautions, a measles epidemic was introduced into the college by cadets returning from holiday. Ultimately there were 127 cases.

As with any large community, the college did not escape the sadness of death. For instance, on the 22nd November 1907 Cadet Captain G.H. Hindson died at Osborne after a short illness. On Monday the 25th the College assembled at 09.20 at the Kingston pontoon. Part of the burial service was read then the coffin was taken aboard the torpedo boat which transferred it to Southampton for the onward journey to its final destination at Penrith. In 1914 the local papers reported an impressive scene at Trinity Wharf when the body of a cadet who had died of pneumonia at the college was conveyed for burial at Guildford. Marines were drawn up on one side of the wharf while blue-jackets carried the coffin to the college steamboat *Beta*.

A Mr Moon asked the East Cowes Urban District Council in 1915 to take action concerning the statements in Parliament regarding the health of cadets at the Royal Naval College. Despite measures being taken to ensure the health of the cadets, in 1917 the national daily papers were agitating against the site of the Osborne college because they considered it unhealthy.

In the churchyard at St Mildred's church at Whippingham, are the graves of five cadets who did not survive their time at Osborne and for some reason were not transferred to their home towns. Three of these died during the measles outbreak of 1917 when over 150 Cadets were ill. On occasions the college would be closed down until an epidemic was under control. A mortuary chapel was built on the Osborne estate for use by the college and convalescent home as required.

Training afloat

The inclusion of land allocated to the College on the eastern bank of the sheltered River Medina allowed a training vessel to be moored there with easy access. This provided practical experience, both of shipboard activities and engineering in a realistic environment. The training vessel also served another practical purpose. Early on in the cadet's time at Osborne they were taken to sea, either in the college vessel or another navy ship operating from Portsmouth, preferably in

HMS Racer at her moorings on the Medina by the engineering works

rough sea conditions, to ascertain whether a cadet suffered from sea sickness and if he could overcome this affliction. Some people, especially with a heightened sense of balance such as a gymnast, cannot cope with the continuous motion of a ship in a rough sea and become ineffective. If a cadet could not overcome sea sickness he had to reassess his future.

HMS *Racer* had been assigned to *HMS Britannia* for sea training for the cadets in 1896. She was classed as a sloop with a displacement tonnage of 970 tons, length 167 feet (51m), a draught of 14 feet (4.3m) and a 2-cylinder compound expansion engine of 850 horsepower. With the start in the reduction of the number of cadets on board *Britannia*, *Racer* was transferred to the Royal Naval College Osborne. A picture of the *Racer* while at *Britannia* shows her with sails set. On leaving the River Dart she went to Portsmouth for a refit then moved to her moorings in the River Medina, without the rigging required for sails! The river bed had to be dredged out to provide sufficient water for her to stay afloat at all states of the tide at her moorings by the workshops. This proved difficult and eventually explosives were used with dramatic results. For accounting purposes RN personnel are assigned to a ship. For standardisation, shore establishments were given a ship's name, so the cap bands of the ratings attached to Osborne carried the name *HMS Racer*. Presumably this practice continued after *HMS Racer* was removed from the Medina in 1916 to be rebuilt as a salvage vessel to recover sunken submarines and other casualties. As such she was classed as a Fleet Auxiliary vessel rather than HMS so both the shore establishment and the vessel carried the same name. Her career was crowned by the recovery, after the end of WWI, of £5 million of bullion from the sunken *Laurentic* off Northern Island. This recovery was led by Lieutenant Commander Guybon Damant, a navy specialist in diving who lived in Cambridge Road, East Cowes.

An early copy of the Osborne College magazine has a photo of another vessel provided for training afloat. She was a second-class cruiser, *HMS Eclipse*, of 5,600 tons fitted with an 8,000 horsepower engine. This would suggest that the low powered *Racer* was used mainly in the Solent and other ships based at Portsmouth were used to take cadets out for experience of the open sea. *Eclipse* was replaced by *HMS Hermes* from 1905 until 1907 when *Hermes* was recommissioned and *Eclipse* resumed her role until 1912. Cadets also had the experience of ocean cruising. The Easter 1908 copy of the college magazine recounts a cruise some of the cadets undertook to the Mediterranean on board *HMS Cornwall*.

The *Racer* started weekly cruising in the Solent area on the first Monday morning after the cadets joined the college in September 1903. Her complement consisted of one lieutenant, two boatswains and one artificer engineer. When the fifteen cadets joined on the Sunday afternoon they were accompanied by one lieutenant, one surgeon and one master. The *Racer* was laid up for the winter on the 18th November 1903 and remained on her moorings until 20th January 1904, when she moved down to White's Yard for minor repairs. On the 6th February she went to Portsmouth to load up with stores, returning on the 11th. An article in the Osborne magazine went on to say *"Cold and wet prevailed and the cadets did not come aboard until the 29th and on the 1st March we made our first voyage for the year which was to Totland Bay, but little enjoyment for anyone, a small ship not being the place for comfort when the thermometer gets below 38 degrees."* These log extracts indicate the activities undertaken during a week's cruise in 1905. *"Tuesday March 14th Day 2 – To the Warner Lightship, blowing from the south west, more seasickness." "Friday 17th March. Engineer Lieutenant Priton took cadets round Dockyard [Portsmouth]. C-in-C met Cadets."* (Commander in Chief)

On the bank of the river near the workshops there was a hauling out slip with a boat house and a one-ton electric winch and a second boat shed and slip.

An example of the boys' physical training while at the college

Learning the principles before going afloat

The quay was built over the remains of a very old stone pier. A legend states that King Charles I landed here on his way to imprisonment at Carisbrooke, hence the name Kingston Farm (King's Stone) on which the works were built. In 1905 a third boat shed was constructed just north of the others.

In addition to sea-going vessels the cadets used boats on the Medina. A ship's whaler was set up on a turntable on the parade ground at the stable block to teach the cadets the basic principles of sailing. Whalers and gigs were provided to teach the cadets sailing and rowing on the Medina. The college also had the use of a Torpedo Boat, number *055*. In 1914 the college had the use of a steamboat named *Beta*. From photographs it appears that during the summer term there was a prize giving ceremony when fond parents visited the college. They were entertained by boat races on the river and a display of physical exercises on the playing fields opposite the officers' accommodation.

The Staff

A naval Captain, Rosslyn Wemyss, was the first to be appointed in overall charge of the college. A separate house was built for him near the officers' accommodation. Naval officers taught naval subjects while civilian teachers taught the normal academic subjects. The officers were supported by some Petty Officers who were also appointed to educate the cadets in engineering and nautical subjects. While these members of the naval staff enjoyed better accommodation than that on board a warship, the philosophy of a ship's company living together was

The staff of Naval Officers with the Prince of Wales when his son Edward joined in 1907

The engineering staff at Kingston Works

The academic staff outside the Cochrane classroom block

maintained by having these men living in the college grounds. As the college later expanded several of the Petty Officers, especially the married ones, were allowed to live in homes around the town. Several families descending from these men live in the town today.

Fisher knew that he needed the best quality officers to run the British Navy. He therefore sought to employ leading academic staff to give the cadets a good grounding in the basic educational subjects. J.A. Ewing, Professor of Mechanical Engineering at Cambridge University, was appointed Director of Naval Education. While the Headmaster had his own office near the classrooms, he and the other teachers lived in accommodation around the Town. Ewing recruited the civilian lecturers, among them Cyril Ashford, the senior science master at Harrow School who was appointed Headmaster. Wemyss and Ashford were to take the first batch of cadets, at the end of their two years at Osborne, on to the new Britannia College to carry through the implementation of the new teaching regime. When this happened in 1905, Wemyss was in charge of both establishments. Charles Godfrey, a mathematician, took Ashford's place at Osborne.

For the first term the Head Master, Cyril Ashford, was supported by nine other teachers teaching English, French, Science and Mathematics. There were five more teachers on the roll for the next term that extended the curriculum to include History. There were nine teaching officers under Captain Wemyss. These included Captain G.L.Raikes from the Royal Military Academy at Woolwich that trained military officers. These were supported by other officers who included a Chaplain, Staff Surgeon and Surgeon, Staff Paymaster and Assistant Pay Master who looked after the college victualling and clothing of the naval staff, a Carpenter Lieutenant and a Gunner. During the first term, Staff Surgeon Robert Hill gave a weekly series of first aid lectures to the staff in the Officers' Mess Room at 9.15. pm after the cadets had turned in. Winter lectures were also started on Saturday evenings.

During the first two years the staff numbers grew as more cadets joined each term. In subsequent years the college magazine recorded a steady change of personnel. Naval personnel were regularly moved from ship to ship and establishment to establishment during their career, compared to the civilian teaching staff. In the Easter 1908 edition it was noted that Lieutenant Saurin who had been Master of the Basset Hounds and Engineer Lieutenant Cox who had been the golf champion were leaving. One wonders whether other members of staff maintained the enthusiasm for those sporting activities.

With the advent of WWI the young naval instructor officers were replaced by some nearing retirement. There were also changes in the civilian staff as some of them enlisted to fight in the armed forces. An indication of the quality of the teaching staff is that Geoffrey Callender joined Osborne in 1905 as a history master. He produced three text books on naval history in 1907, 1909 and 1911 that were used at both Osborne and Britannia. He also designed the programmes for a number of the Christmas pantomimes performed by the cadets and staff. He was one of the earliest members of the Society for Nautical Research that was founded in 1910. In 1920 he became Honorary Secretary and treasurer of the Society. When Osborne closed he joined the staff at Britannia but left in 1922 to become Professor of History at the Royal Naval College Greenwich. He used his position in the Society for Nautical Research to cause it to be instrumental in saving HMS Victory for the nation in 1922. Subsequently he became the first Director of the National Maritime Museum at Greenwich.

The Cadets

The admittance of young men at the age of thirteen to start their training to become naval officers was governed by their passing a written examination, an interview at the Admiralty in London and a medical examination. To a certain

Term photo taken on the Cricket Pavilion steps

A Cadet's sea chest, his only wardrobe

extent it was also governed by the parents' ability to cover the costs. The fees were £25 per term with an initial outlay on uniform. In addition to their best uniform there were work and sports clothes. Serving on board ship required a considerable wardrobe to cater for the different climates one would experience. For a naval cadet there was even more personal equipment that, as he progressed through his career, would accompany him. All his kit was contained in a wooden sea chest strong enough to withstand the roughest handling by the seamen assisting his transportation in joining and leaving each ship.

The company of Gieve, Matthews & Seagrove, with their head office in London, provided many naval officers with their uniform. They had three branches in Portsmouth, one in Chatham, one in Weymouth and one in Devonport. The company managed to capture the market in supplying the cadets with their outfits. They obviously valued the business highly as they published their own book entitled *"How to become a Naval Officer"*. This book contains all that the parents of an aspiring admiral would need to know to send their son on his way. The list of equipment covers two pages as it also includes bedding, toiletry equipment, laundry bag and the sports clothing that was worn. Like any boarding school, the Navy were well aware of the need to encourage a teenager's healthy development, especially because, as still applies today, a seafarer needs to be as healthy as possible. Sports activities featured largely in the weekly routine.

The suppliers did not want to frighten off potential parents so the final section of *"How to become a Naval Officer"* lists the rates of pay their sons could expect. It starts with the Admiral of the Fleet being paid £2190 a year in 1907, plus all the allowances such as Table Money for the admirals, Command money, plus payment for navigation, gunnery or torpedo duties and acting pay when carrying out duties of a superior rank.

Having got through the entrance procedure, each new cadet was sent his uniform to travel in to Portsmouth. Usually his sea chest had been delivered to the college a week earlier. He joined the other cadets in their trains from various parts of the country and disembarked at the station on Victoria Quay in Portsmouth Dockyard. The new entrants embarked on board a navy vessel to transport them to the strange island seen mistily across the water.

This was the start of the long process of training a Royal Navy Officer who had to function efficiently while the enemy tried to sink his ship and he to sink the enemy. The Cadets spent two years at Osborne. By the time the first entry into Osborne had completed their two years, the Britannia College at Dartmouth had been completed. The Osborne cadets then moved to the Britannia College for a further two years followed by eight months on board a cruiser. After successfully completing the Passing Out examination the cadets served three years as a midshipman. After passing another examination in navigation, steam engineering and general subjects this was followed by eight months of gunnery, torpedo and pilotage courses at Greenwich. At the age of twenty one they could become a sub-lieutenant serving at sea for a year before finally deciding whether to specialise and enter one of the branches for engineering, gunnery, torpedo, navigation, or marines, or to serve as general service lieutenants. At this stage the engineers went to the engineering college at Keyham at Devonport. The result of this was that, as time passed, all naval officers would have a comprehensive grounding in all the disciplines required to operate a man-of-war in a common setting of strict discipline.

On arrival at East Cowes the new cadets landed at Trinity Wharf, marched up the hill and entered the grounds of the college, from which they emerged only to march down to the engineering workshops at Kingston and during free time on Sunday afternoons. The shops in the Town were "out of bounds". As a concession cadets were allowed to receive friends in the college on Sunday afternoons.

From the start the cadets were steeped in naval tradition with each term being assigned the name of an historic admiral and each dormitory being similarly named. Louis Mountbatten recounted his arrival in 1913 in a letter to his parents – *"I arrived at Portsmouth only just in time. The station master met me. We were inspected on the jetty. I was photographed twice by reporters. It was a nice rough crossing. Our twenty strong term is called the Exmouth Term. My dormitory is called Howe. My bunk is the second on the right on entering the dormitory. My Class is the Starboard Watch. Our term officer is Lieutenant Matby."* The regulation about not going into the town was probably waived for Mountbatten as his father, the recently retired Admiral of the Fleet Prince Louis of Battenberg, was living part of the time down the hill in Kent House in York Avenue. Many of the young men joining as cadets came from wealthy families. Some had had their own tutors and were not used to school life. So the daily regime must have come to all of them as an unpleasant shock.

Life at the College

The bugle call for lunch

Life was governed by bugle calls. In the winter the first was Reveille at 06.30. However some cadets may have been awake earlier when the naval seaman on the night watch came in at 05.00 to put a match to the fire in the stove. The huts, constructed of timber frames clad in two layers of Uralite with asbestos packing between and a large window between each bunk, were not warm. The Uralite was so weak that cadets could put holes in the walls with their elbows. Reveille triggered a mad rush of cadets stripping off their pyjamas, rushing down the dorm to the plunge pool for a quick dip in cold water, getting dressed and consuming a cup of hot cocoa – all in 30 minutes.

At 07.00 the cadets started their studies for 45 minutes. Then there was breakfast for 40 minutes. At 08.50 the cadets mustered for Divisions and prayers, probably in the large Hall of Nelson block. From 09.00 there were classes. The cadets were divided into two groups, those studying in the classrooms in St

Cadets emerging from Crossways Road

Vincent or the Cochrane Building and those going to the workshops for practical training. There the cadets learned the skills that were needed to maintain a warship at sea. There was a break during the morning for milk in the mess

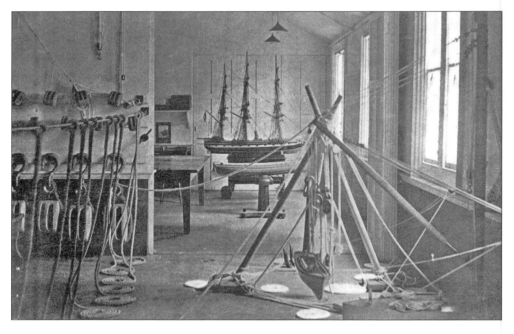

The seamanship room

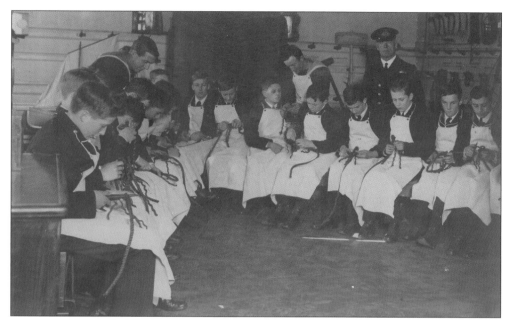

Splicing practice

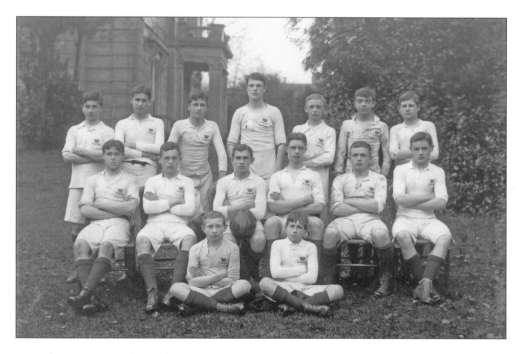

A rugby team outside Park House

Nelson Hall in use as a gymnasium

Swimming from the pier in Osborne Bay

The tennis courts and cricket nets near the Officers' Quarters

room. Lunch was taken between 13.10 and 13.40. After lunch the two groups of cadets changed over between academic and practical studies. Studies finished at 16.30 when there was another milk break and the cadets then changed into appropriate clothes for sporting activities. At 18.30 the cadets changed for supper which lasted half an hour. Studies resumed at 19.45 for half an hour. Evening prayers were held in Nelson at 20.45 then the cadets turned in at 21.00.

In line with the Selborne Scheme's intention to produce healthy as well as educated officers, there was a lot of sport played by the Cadets. Wednesday and Saturday afternoons were completely given over to sports. To a certain extent the amount of each sport undertaken depended on the personal interest and skills of the officers and staff. The sporting activities included most of those enjoyed at any public school - Football, Hockey, Cricket, Rugby, cross country running or following the college Basset Hounds. In addition there were gymnastics, fencing and boxing. During the summer, tides permitting, a bathing party mustered at 17.30 outside the dormitories, marched down to Osborne Bay and returned an hour later. The original golf course and club house were restored and the course enlarged during the first term in 1903.

The list below is an example of the limited interschool activity as shown in the college magazine.

During the Easter term of 1904 there were four hockey matches:-

On January 25th the cadets played the Vikings at Newport and won 5 to 3,

On February 4th they played Redbridge at home and won 4 to 1,

On March 1st they played Sea Field Park College at home and won 6 to 5,

On March 4th they played the Royal Naval College Portsmouth at Portsmouth and lost 1 to 8.

There were several football fixtures that term.

On January 28th the cadets played Mr Crookshanks school at football at Osborne and won 10 to nil.   Against Stubbington House the 1st XI lost 0-8, the 2nd XI won 2-1 and the A team lost 1-4.

On February 18th they played Mr Helbut's team from Winchester at home and won 13-0.

However during that term the only outside rugby match was the 2nd XV against Mr Crookshank's School at Lee-on-Solent on the March 1st which the college won easily.

This timetable meant that the cadets spent about 45% of their instruction time on normal scholastic subjects, 33% of their time on engineering and 21% engaged in sport. This ratio epitomised the intent of the Selbourne training scheme.

Divisions in the Nelson Hall

A mast from a naval ship was set up to fly the white ensign. Rigging was set up which the cadets climbed to accustom them to heights. A safety net was fitted that proved its worth.

Sunday morning was taken up with Divisions and a church service in Nelson. In the autumn of 1907 a small chapel was built on the eastern end of the Nelson Block between that building and the first of the dormitories, Hawke. It was fitted out with various items presented to the college – a brass eagle lectern, a brass alter cross, a silver chalice and paten, a burse and vail for communion and a brass plaque in memory of Cadet Fare. The Sunday morning services were regularly addressed by leaders of the Church of England. During the winter 07—08 these included several Bishops, the chaplain of the RN College Britannia and a senior chaplain for The Mission to Seamen. On March 22nd it was the turn of the Bishop of Winchester who confirmed 50 cadets of the sixth term. The collection that day was on behalf of the Osborne Chapel Fund and raised £12-9-2d. Donations were being given to the Chapel. A silver flagon was presented by the parents of Cadet Captain Hindson who had died at Osborne on the 22nd November 1907. An inscribed brass plaque in memory of Cadet B.H. Carew who had died at Osborne on the 15th May 1906 was presented by his sister. The visits by Bishops to confirm cadets in the Anglican faith continued. In the spring of

A short pause in the routine

1920 the Bishop of Winchester visited to confirm 76 cadets. The church organ that was installed in Nelson still exists and is in use in the Methodist Chapel in Adelaide Grove, East Cowes.

On Sunday afternoons the cadets were allowed to go out of the college until 1800. The Commandant of the Convalescent Home was very protective of the tranquillity around the House so the cadets were restricted in the use of the grounds. On the east side of the house they were required to keep to the Valley Walk when going down to the beach for their swimming.

In 1876, when the Admiralty were considering sites for a shore-based training establishment, comment was made that proximity to a naval port would be an advantage. When the Osborne naval college was built it would appear that its location provided the cadets with opportunities for such things as visits to naval ships, to help them understand the future life they would be leading. They were taken on visits to the shipbuilding yards of J S White in East Cowes and the naval shipyard in Portsmouth where Dreadnought battleships were being built. The cadets were amazed at the complexity and noise of the work being carried out to create warships.

Another development in 1907 was the creation of a band. On learning that a foreign potentate was likely to visit the college, it was decided to train a band and drill the cadets to march to the tune of its martial strains. The potentate did not appear but the band continued and flourished. With Royal Marines among the college staff the band may have benefited from superior tuition. By the summer of 1908, when the Prince and Princess of Wales paid a weekend visit, there was a march past on the Sunday morning after the church service and the band showed that they had improved out of all recognition.

At the end of the summer term in 1914, just as the cadets and staff were preparing to go home for the summer leave, the Admiralty decided that the political situation required them to test the Navy's preparedness for conflict. The Cadets and some staff were appointed to several of the large fleet of warships that carried out a weekend of manoeuvres in the English Channel. At the end of the trials the cadets did not go home because, on the 28th July war was declared and the country went into a state of war. During World War One there was such a shortage of manpower for the Royal Navy ships that a number of cadets did not go on to Britannia but were sent to sea on completing their training at Osborne. A considerable number of these cadets were killed at the battle of Jutland at the end of May 1916.

Royal Naval College Osborne Cadet Entries

YEAR	JAN	MAY	SEPT	TOTAL	
1903			72	72	
1904	72	76	66	214	
1905	86	64	78	228	
1906	70	79	63	212	
1907	71	67	64	202	Prince Edward entered May
1908	68	66	66	200	
1909	75	68	71	214	Prince Albert entered Jan. Prince Edward left April
1910	76	68	73	217	Prince Albert left Dec.
1911	75	76	68	219	
1912	77	78	74	229	
1913	77	76	70	223	Louis Mountbatten (Battenberg) entered May
1914	60	52	101	213	
1915	122	104	110	336	Louis Mountbatten (Battenberg) left April
1916	104	105	104	313	Prince George entered Sept.
1917	99	105	99	303	
1918	95	85	77	257	Prince George left July
1919	77	37	40	154	
1920	39	39	41	119	
1921	42			42	
TOTAL				3967	

The numbers show that the college was full until 1919

The Peace Dividend

From the time the college was opened in 1903 there was expansion and improvement until its maximum period of activity during WWI. With the end of hostilities came the consequences of peacetime budget requirements. The fleet was rapidly reduced by the selling or scrapping of older redundant ships and decommissioning of others into the reserve fleet. During the War the number of cadets starting their training rose to a maximum of 336 in 1915. By 1918 it was down to 257. By this time Britannia was well established with plenty of accommodation that had been added in 1907 and 1917 and could cater for the needs of the Navy in peace time. The intake at Osborne declined, until, in 1921 it was only 42. The decision was made that the temporary creation of the Royal Naval College Osborne had served its purpose and was no longer required. By the end of 1921 it was closed. The records and trophies were transferred to Britannia Naval College at Dartmouth.

However the impact of the training at Osborne lived on. Among the 3,967 cadets who passed through the College at East Cowes were members of royal and eminent families as well as some of the most talented youngsters of that time. In 1939, when Britain went to war with Germany again, the boys who had trained at Osborne were aged between 31 and 49. These officers were the backbone of the Royal Navy that helped to win victory. King George VI had started his career at Osborne and was proud to wear his naval uniform.

The Osborne House Stable Block was now about to enter the next phase of its complex history.

CHAPTER FIVE

1921 – 1939
Uses made of the College buildings and grounds

Discussion on the Disposal of the Naval College buildings

When the Admiralty decided to leave Osborne and accommodate all the boys at Britannia, the question arose of what should happen to the extensive buildings at Osborne. The outlay value had been £147,000 at the Stable Block site, £16,000 at the Hospital and £33,000 at the Workshops. It was felt that the value in 1921 should be doubled because of inflation. There were no other naval purposes for which the buildings were required.

The Treasury would not sanction money for demolition as that would cost £10,000. They wanted the Office of Works to formulate a definite scheme for the disposal of the property. The comment was made, *"It seems incredible that some use cannot be made of it."*

By the end of June 1923 the Admiralty had removed all the equipment from the college buildings on the Osborne Estate, apart from the potato peeler. The Admiralty no longer had any connection with the stable block which passed back to the Ministry of Works. While uses were being sought for the stable block, the public continued to visit the staterooms of Osborne House as they had from 1904. There was still no vehicular access for coaches carrying visitors, so parking was restricted to the main road.

Post WWI government cuts made the reuse of equipment a logical step. The Army Council had expressed an interest in using the premises for training, but then abandoned the idea.

The Power station under construction in 1918 next to the old college workshops

It was hoped that the Local Authority would take on the Isolation Hospital, but they already had one. It was felt the engineering works by the river should be sold for commercial use. All the equipment inside had been removed to other Naval establishments.

In the autumn of 1921 the Petty Officers Quarters were taken on as staff accommodation for the Osborne Convalescent Home. This situation continued until the year 2000, when the Convalescent Home closed. In 2001 the Petty Officers Quarters were converted by English Heritage into a refreshment room,

The Petty Officers Quarters

shop and ticket office. There are a few photographs depicting life at the Naval College on the walls of the refreshment room. At the same time the old sick bay, opposite the Petty Officers Quarters, for the Marines and seamen based at the college was converted into a toilet block.

The cricket pavilion and cricket field were used by various people, such as Maurice Myram, a local landlord at the Victoria Tavern in Clarence

Flower beds by the Petty Officers quarters when used by Convalescent Home staff

Road, who formed a cricket team, and the Groves and Guttridge cricket team. In 1933, when it was suggested the pavilion should be demolished, Hubert Saunders offered to rebuild it. He was a Director of the East Cowes shipbuilding firm of Groves and Guttridge and was using the sports facilities for the younger personnel of the firm, paying 16 shillings and 8 pence a month. During WWII the field was used for potatoes. By 2018 the cricket pavilion had been converted by English Heritage and is let out as self-catering accommodation.

The College cricket pavilion in 2018

The remaining bases of the dormitories are now buried under concrete

The suggestion was made that the Naval College buildings could be turned into a borstal, but in 1931 the Prison Commission decided they were unsuitable. Another idea was that it could be used for the criminally insane, but it was pointed out that holes could be easily kicked in the walls of the dormitory blocks.

In September 1933 it was decided that the temporary Uralite buildings should be demolished. They had become a white elephant. A demolition firm from London started work in October 1933, using the officers' mess as their accommodation and office. An entrance from the main road was created past the water towers at this time. Demolition material was sold from the site. By March 1935 all the demolition of these buildings was complete, leaving just the concrete foundations showing the positions of the dormitories, officer accommodation, the Nelson Block, the science laboratory and Headmaster's office.

Many visitors to Osborne House arrived by coach or charabanc. From 1935 these motorised coaches entered the grounds by the entrance used today by visitors to Vectis Storage and DHL. The coaches drove around the Stable Block and entered the central courtyard through the archway. The passengers disembarked and walked to the House past the great wooden doors. The coaches parked in the courtyard awaiting the return of their passengers.

The visitors' car park for Osborne House in 2019 shows the great area that had been covered by the dormitories. The water towers and the Cochrane building remained, and the Stable Block, called St. Vincent then Collingwood in Naval College days, was left standing proudly, looking as it was in 1921.

Before the dormitories were demolished several uses were made of the old college buildings and grounds.

Uses of the Stable Block 1921 to 1939

A Holiday Camp

In 1921 the Office of Works stated, *"It is possible that some enterprising syndicate might be found to establish a holiday camp or something similar."* In October 1925 there was a proposal by a Major Sandes of Allnatt Ltd., to use the buildings as a kind of convalescent home for elementary school children, who would be taught at the same time. There was discussion on heating and fencing that might be required for this, and as long as the lessee paid for the fencing it was agreed this should go ahead in 1926. There would be no rent for the first year, £250 payable for the second year and £750 thereafter. Various agreements were made with the Governor of Osborne House and the King also agreed to the scheme. However, by November 1926 there was doubt if the convalescent scheme for children would ever take off.

Instead, in 1927 Allnatts took out a lease on the Naval College Isolation Hospital blocks opposite Barton Manor for a holiday camp, and in 1928 Mr Allnutt was given a lease on just the three southern dormitory blocks of the Naval College when he needed extra accommodation for his holiday camp.

By 1930 Mr Allnatt offered to buy the whole Naval College site, but only if he could have direct access to the sea, which was refused. The following year he suggested using the place for foreign university students, mostly German and Austrian. There was much correspondence about this, but it was felt that the site was too small for the 800 students envisaged, and it was doubted if Allnatt had the financial backing required for the project. He continued to run the Hospital site successfully as a holiday camp until 1939. Customers included some groups of the Hitler Youth Movement, who used to march, singing as they went, down to East Cowes beach to swim. Other holidaymakers were groups of apprentices

THE EAST COWES HOLIDAY CAMP, I.O.W.

Proprietors: ALLNATT, LTD.

Registered Offices: Chase Estate, Park Royal Road, N. Acton, N.W.10.

Telephone: COWES 274.   Manager: G. L. OLDHAM.

from industrial firms, one of them being Guest, Keene and Nettlefold (GKN) who occupy the Hospital site in 2019.

Red Cross Voluntary Aid Detachment Training Camps at Osborne 1927 to 1933

The Island branch of the Red Cross was set up in 1910 under the Presidency of Princess Beatrice, with the first Red Cross Voluntary Aid Detachment (VAD) nurse registered in 1911. At this time the rising threat of German aggression led to the formation of the Territorial Army of volunteers. Also the expansion of the Red Cross was deemed essential as there would be a shortage of nurses should war commence. Voluntary Aid Detachments for both men and women were set up to work alongside military nurses. The VAD role was to provide nursing and medical assistance during time of war.

Training camps in 1913 and 1914 were held at Newtown rifle camp and by the summer of 1914 there were 175 men and 341 women under training on the Island. During WWI many VADS did nursing duty at the Island's auxiliary hospitals such as Northwood House at Cowes and Gatcombe House south of Newport. Over 11,000 military patients were brought to the Island to be treated at the Auxiliary hospitals. Princess Beatrice made frequent visits to the wounded. The VAD nurses continued with their training after the end of WWI.

In 1979 Miss Cynthia Stocker stayed at Osborne House for a short period of convalescence. She reminisced about her experiences as a VAD nurse, working at the training camps in the Osborne Naval College buildings and grounds from 1927 to 1933. The Convalescent House Governor in 1979, Surgeon Commander

VAD camp using the college buildings

Navy during WWI and was a bandsman at the Royal Naval College, Osborne before its closure in 1921.

In 1933 Admiral of the Fleet Earl Jellicoe visited the Osborne Sea Cadet Corps at Osborne Stable Block to inspect them. From the photographs, there were more than fifty boys and ten officers. During WWII many of these boys were serving in the Royal Navy, benefitting from their initial training at Osborne Stable Block.

The boys had drill, gymnastics and rifle training, as well as general nautical training and a band. They also had a gun on a carriage and towed this around the streets of East Cowes on occasions. Ernest Oatley remembered an event at a ladies garden party at Barton Manor where they wanted the Cadets to do a gun display. Mr Frank Thomas, DSM, ex-naval gunners mate, pointed out that it would not do the lawn much good, but they were asked to fire the gun. Everyone was seated facing the Cadets as the powder was put into the friction tube and when the gun fired everyone jumped in surprise. It wrecked the lawn but the boys got a huge round of applause!

In the mid-1930s the majority of the Osborne College buildings, including the Nelson Hall, were dismantled, so the Sea Cadets moved into what had once been the carriage house, converted in 1903 into the dining room for the college boys. This became known as the Osborne Hall and there were activities for the Sea Cadets every night, with a couple of billiard tables there too.

Navy League Sea Cadets

Gym display in the Courtyard

Field Gun training

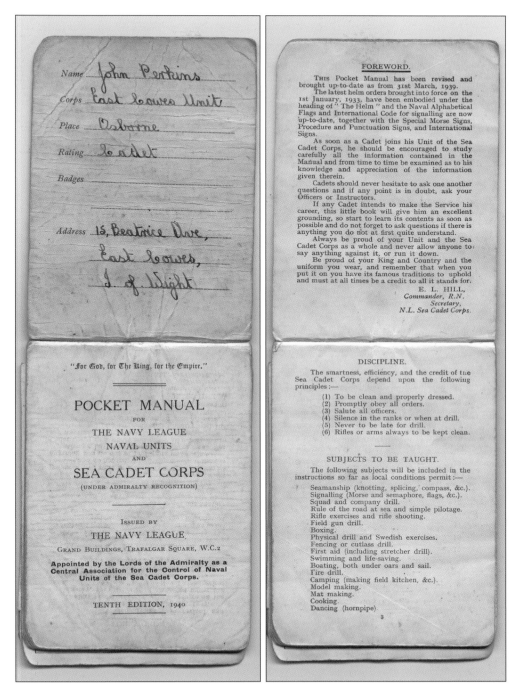

A Cadet's pocket book

A 15 ton yawl was given to the Cadets in about 1935, called *Nyama*. A minimum of six Sea Cadets were needed to sail the boat, which they took all around the Solent. In 1942 she was moored in the river near the power station when the major blitz on the town took place but only the top of her mast was broken. However the sails were all stored in Marvin's shed, together with the rigging. That shed burnt out in the blitz and the Corps could not afford to replace the sails so *Nyama* was sold.

When Saunders Roe requisitioned the Osborne Hall in 1940, the Osborne Sea Cadets moved on to a two masted schooner, the *Mabel Taylor*, moored on a mud berth in East Cowes. Later she was moved to west Cowes but the vessel was condemned in 1954. In 1958 premises were built at Whitegates, Artic Road, west Cowes and the unit continued to flourish. They have recently built new headquarters on the site, and proudly keep the title *TS Osborne (Cowes Sea Cadets)* in 2019.

CHAPTER SIX

1939 – 1948
The impact of WWII
on the old stable block

Air Raid Precautions (ARP) store

From plans of the stable block annotated in 1940 showing who was using the building, we see that the Air Raid Precautions established at East Cowes had set up ARP mobilisation stores here. These were housed in the large set of classrooms, previously stables, to the north of the archway. The stairs are included in the plans, so the stores probably included the upstairs room, the old library, as well. This would have given the ARP a considerable space to store emergency food rations, emergency bedding and first aid equipment etc. This equipment could then be distributed to wherever it was required.

The First Aid Post in the town was based at the East Cowes Town Hall. They realised in 1942 that this was vulnerable to enemy bombing as the nearby shipyards were destroyed in May that year. The First Aid post was then moved to Crossways House, across the road from the Stable Block. The main East Cowes ARP base was at Kent House in York Avenue.

World War II ARP badge

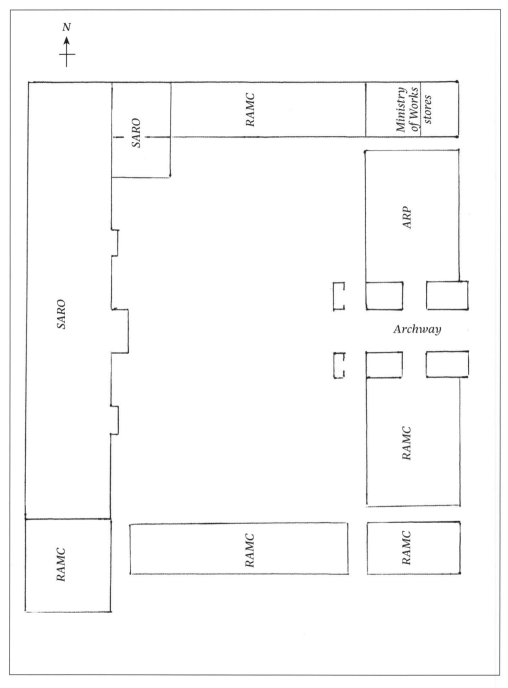

Organisations using the stable block 1940

The Royal Army Medical Corps (RAMC) 1940 – 1944

The 12th Field Ambulance Brigade moved into part of the Osborne Stable Block and the Cochrane building of the old Naval College on 27th June 1940 as they urgently required accommodation on the Island. They also occupied Barton Manor, the adjacent estate to the south of Osborne. The large unit consisted of 400 Officers and other ranks. Their equipment included a field hospital, tents, etc., plus 41 motor vehicles ranging from ambulances to motor cycles. The vehicles needed to be concealed from enemy planes, possibly beneath the trees. The old stable block was deemed suitable because it had access to the main road, was isolated from the rest of the Osborne estate and had water and latrines. By 4th July 1940 they had also set up numerous tents.

The RAMC did not have the use of the old Carriage House. This had been used by the Sea Cadets until June 1940, when Saunders Roe had requisitioned this part of the Stable Block urgently for storage of aircraft parts. The ARP had the ground and first floor rooms on the north side of the archway. The RAMC used the whole of the Cochrane Block as their hospital. Toilets were added to the east side of the Cochrane building. Part of the Stable Block was used by the RAMC for dental care for the troops.

Barton Manor was their Headquarters and was also used as a hospital for 20 officer patients. The officers of the RAMC were billeted there. The Commanding Officer was Lt. Col. W. M. Cameron.

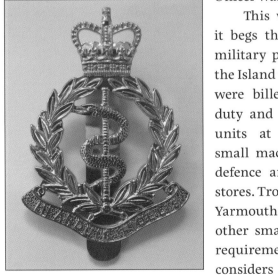

Royal Army Medical Corps

This was a large unit of the RAMC so it begs the question, where were all these military patients coming from? From 1939 the Island was heavily defended. Many troops were billeted on the Island for protective duty and training. There were anti-aircraft units at Whippingham and Nettlestone, small machine gun emplacements for local defence around the Island plus munitions stores. Troops were based at Fort Victoria near Yarmouth and Puckpool Battery at Ryde and other smaller sites. There were even more requirements for medical services when one considers the troops training on the Island. Accidents frequently happen during training.

Barton Manor – Officers' Quarters and hospital from 1940 to 1945

Canadian troops housed at East Cowes Castle and Scottish troops also in the area were preparing for the Dieppe raid in 1942. There was mention of a Canadian medical corps based on the Island as well. The Royal Marine Commandos 40 and 41 units were based at Bembridge, Sandown and Chale. Later, there were many tank landing craft crews training for the Normandy invasion. In 1944 there were massive camps of troops training on the north coast of the Island and awaiting embarkation on the Normandy invasion fleet. The flow of traffic carrying army personnel who needed treatment at the Stable Block must have been considerable.

We know that sick Prisoner of War officers were accommodated at Barton Manor. On one occasion, a German officer was being carried by stretcher from Barton to the hospital unit in the Cochrane building when a German plane came over, firing its machine guns. The officer was unceremoniously dumped on the ground and the stretcher party dived for cover!

The Royal Navy had a number of bases on the Island. These personnel had the facilities of Haslar hospital at Gosport available but emergency first aid treatment for them may have been at Osborne. So, once again, the old Victorian stable block proved to be an important asset to the Island. There was at least one other RAMC Unit, based on the Island, at Totland, in 1944.

The RAMC were still in occupation at the Stable Block in 1944 on D-day. One of the East Cowes ARP First Aid Ambulances had to go to the RAMC at Osborne that morning and the East Cowes First Aiders received tea from a very strong brew, complete with added sugar! Some of this unit of RAMC may have moved to France soon after D-day. Certainly by January 1945 Saunders Roe were planning a take over of all of the Stable Block.

Saunders Roe Ltd

By 1908 Sam Saunders' business of constructing fast motor boats was growing. He moved from Cowes to East Cowes to get better facilities purchasing a site on the foreshore at the bottom of Old Road called the Columbine Yard. In 1909 he formed a second company *"to build everything required for aero-navigation"*. During WWI his company built over 400 planes on Government contracts, mainly seaplanes, at his aircraft works close to the Folly Inn on the east bank of the River Medina at Whippingham. These seaplanes were planes whose wings were supported by floats for landing on water. Saunders used his boatbuilding expertise to design planes whose hull was built as a boat, a flying-boat. These were constructed using his patented strong "Consuta" plywood. This allowed much larger aircraft to be built that could land on water. Much of the company's manufacturing was based on its experience of plywood. Post WWI the company were designing and building commercial seaplanes and flying boats. Sam Saunders retired in 1928. Sir Alliot Verdon Roe had sold his aircraft building business a few years before. On Saunders' retirement A. V. Roe bought his company and called it Saunders Roe Ltd. In 1935 the company greatly enlarged the Columbine Works in anticipation of government military contracts.

WWII was the time when the Saunders Roe company started to use the old Stable Block. On 25th June 1940 a letter was sent by Mr J Nelson, secretary at Saunders Roe, to the Secretary, HM Office of Works. *"I am directed to ask that the unoccupied building at Osborne (to the west of that*

Saunders Roe Lapel badge

used as ARP mobilisation stores,) may be made available in connection with the 1A priority aircraft production, as it may be essential to our needs." (Work 15/75 3N1316 National Archives)

This is the first reference to Saunders Roe at the Stable Block. Two days later, the director of Lands and Accommodation visited the Stable Block and went over the buildings with Captain Clarke, the Managing Director of Saunders Roe. The old carriage house building, then known as Osborne Hall, was required mainly for storage but there might also be a certain amount of fitting together of parts. One or two new entrances to the buildings would need to be made at the rear of the building so that trucks would not need to enter the courtyard.

The old carriage house had been used very successfully by the T.S. Osborne Sea Cadets as their drill hall since the 1930s. On 8th October 1940 when Saunders Roe were given permission to take over the Osborne Hall they agreed to help find the Sea Cadets somewhere else to train. The firm also offered to be responsible for keeping a watch and fire-fighting at the building. An air raid shelter was constructed on the west side of the old carriage house together with a static water supply and store for a mobile pump. Additional buildings were built during the war period. One was a *"Robin Hanger"* that was south of the Cochrane building and east of the long toilet block, on the site of the large college building Nelson. A *"Belfast"* building was constructed on the site of the naval college servants' block between the carriage house and the main road.

The Carriage House after the Blitz of 4th/5th May 1942

Use of the carriage house suffered a blow when the towns of East and west Cowes experienced severe bombing on the night of 4th/5th May 1942. The roofs of the Osborne Hall and rooms to the north of the courtyard were completely destroyed, and it must have burnt out any goods stored within them. It is doubtful whether the building was immediately repaired as plans in early 1945 show the whole damaged area shaded in red.

Dispersal of the Company's Head Office and Works Office to Melchet Court near Romsey and the design team and its test facilities to Beaumaris in Anglesey took place in September 1940. Later that year some aircraft production moved to Addlestone in Surrey.

Wartime production at East Cowes included many *Walrus* and *Sea Otter* amphibious aeroplanes. Saunders Roe were also sub-contractors for major components, which included *Hurricane* and *Spitfire* rudders. By the end of 1944 Saunders Roe was trying to re-establish itself in the field of flying boat design and manufacture. Since 1942 the management had authorised investigation into what aircraft types would be required for civil aviation when the war ended.

The Prisoner of War Camp – Osborne 1945-1948

With the end of hostilities the Office of Works considered what action needed to be taken at the Stable Block. Osborne House was continuing in its role of convalescent home for Service personnel. Mr Barker from the Office of Works, and Mr Pledge, architect, held a meeting at Osborne from 6th to the 8th July 1945 to discuss various matters relating to the Osborne Estate.

At the end of WWII there were many Prisoners of War (POWs) of various nationalities who could not be repatriated immediately to their home countries. Work was found for them in Britain, while they stayed in purpose built camps. Following Mr Barker's visit, he submitted the following memorandum. *"We are contemplating establishing a (POW) camp at Osborne for the joint use of the Ministry of Agriculture and Fisheries and ourselves for agricultural and arboricultural work and generally tidying up the place after much damage by tanks during the war. It is possible that we might also use them to dig up some of the foundations of the Osborne Royal Naval College to provide hardcore for the sea defences and simultaneously to remove a considerable eyesore to the visiting public. Osborne is to re-open to the visiting public on August Bank Holiday [1945]. Would you have any objection to this from your point of view? I presume that you do not require any P.O.W. labour for housing in the Isle of Wight?"*

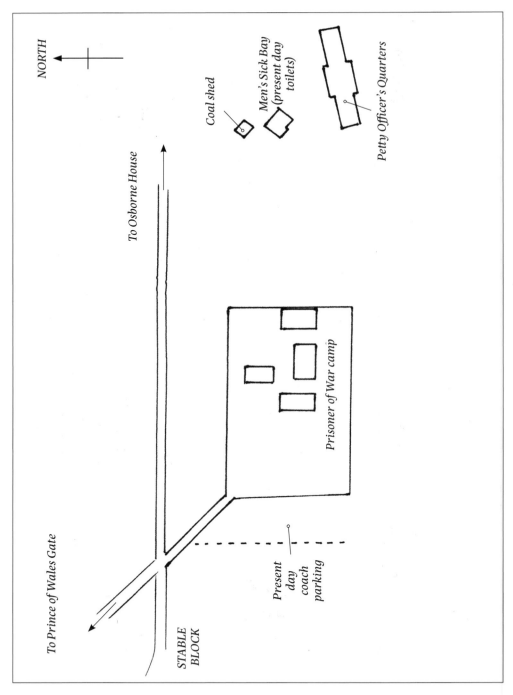

Site of Prisoner of War camp 1946

The answer came back quickly: *"I am very agreeable to erecting a POW Camp for 100 men for your use and would be glad if I could borrow some when a housing site in Cowes is required..."*

The POWs arrived at Osborne from 26th September 1945. Fifty of the men started work on the Osborne Estate College Meadow potato field on 1st October 1945, lifting the potato crop. The remaining fifty were employed by the Ministry of Agriculture in the district. Four of the prisoners were soon in use helping to get the Osborne golf course back into shape. The foundations of the Old College remained undisturbed as there were more immediate tasks requiring their attention.

By March 1946 the soldiers looking after the prisoners of war were planning to create a new road into the estate for the use of the POWs. *"We do not want the POWs to be mixed up with the visiting public in the summer more than is absolutely necessary."* However it was decided that a wide gap in the hedge on road from the Stable Block to the House should be used instead. Today this is the entrance to the Osborne visitors' car park. Arrangements were made that the POWs entered and left at times that did not conflict with visitors.

By July 1946, experience had taught the Osborne Estate staff that they needed to supervise the POWs work efficiently. They could only manage 25 prisoners working on the estate at a time. The camp was still in tents and it was suggested that, if the men were to remain during the winter, Nissen or similar huts should be provided. The foundations of the old dormitories would serve this purpose and there was main drainage on site. This was not the case at another camp in the town between Beatrice Avenue and Gort Road, so that camp was disbanded and the men moved to the more permanent camp at Osborne, built on foundations more than 100 feet from the road to the House.

In August 1946 it was again agreed that the remaining foundations of the old Naval College buildings between the road to the House and the camp should be dug up to provide material to repair the sea wall in Osborne Bay. It was suggested that a pneumatic drill should be hired to break the concrete. The remainder of the foundations of the dormitory blocks, etc, should be planted with coniferous trees, as the concrete was only thin, with a base of gravel below.

In November, the number of prisoners was increased to 150, and their encampment enlarged towards the cricket field. 100 of the men were agricultural workers. The huts still had to be built, but they were quick to erect. Some were occupied by December 13th 1946 and the rest by January 15th 1947.

Quite a number of the prisoners of war had established friendships with local people through the attendance at Church Services in the town, Prisoners visited local people's homes at Christmas and sang carols. Gifts were made by the prisoners and given to these friends at Christmas, such as a

A tea tray made as a Christmas present in 1946

painted wooden tray which has been donated to the East Cowes Heritage Centre.

By July 1947 the "prisoners" were allowed much more freedom and roamed all over the Osborne Estate. There were complaints as to their behaviour. *"They have denuded the Osborne Estate of benches for the benefit of their camp and other convenient articles, and steps must be taken to recover them!"* Meeting freely roaming prisoners was objectionable for the visiting public and the resident patients at the convalescent home. Major General R Priest was the House Governor of Osborne. He was most anxious that the camp should be closed down at the earliest possible date and the Nissen Huts should be removed.

In February 1948, it was decided that until the prisoners could be repatriated they should be moved to Northwood Military Camp between Cowes and Newport. This was taken on loan from the War Department. However it was not until the 14th April 1948 that the hostel for POWs at Osborne was finally closed down.

Some material from the Naval College foundations was taken to the beach and the wall in front of the Queen's Alcove was repaired using it. A strip adjacent to the road to the house was cleared of foundations.

The foundations within the Saunders Roe leased land were not affected, according to the 1940's correspondence. The plunge pool uncovered in 2006 had only suffered superficial damage. The remains of the other nine plunge pools may still exist below the children's playground.

CHAPTER SEVEN

1945 – 1987
Post War use of the Stable Block

Saunders Roe, British Hovercraft Corporation and Westland Aircraft

In the life of the Stable Block, the company of Saunders Roe and its successors figure as the longest continuous users. Consequently it is felt necessary to give suitable space to record the achievements of those designers and other staff who worked at the building during more than 42 years.

For simplicity in this book we are using the one term, Saunders Roe, up to the time Westland Aircraft Ltd became involved. While the company diversified over the years creating a wide range of manufactured products, we are concentrating on the main ones that emanated from the Stable Block drawing offices. With the end of WWII Saunders Roe could bring together at East Cowes the aircraft design team that had been dispersed to Beaumaris on Anglesey, Melchett Court at Romsey and Addlestone in Surrey. The complete reorganisation of the company's facilities at East Cowes was necessary for continued development of the company as a flying boat manufacturer.

Plans drawn up in January 1945 by Saunders Roe showed what alterations they wanted to make to the whole stable block building and the Cochrane Building and associated land, 60,000 square feet in all. This would accommodate their drawing offices and managerial staff. The stable block was to house all the design team and the tracers, the library, print room, technical publications, and the aerodynamics and stress and weights departments. New roof trusses were to be made over the damaged parts of the building, i.e. the old carriage house and northern section of the quadrangle. This provided a large space for a lofting facility to permit the laying out of proposed sections of aircraft.

The Cochrane building, of the Naval college era, was to house the senior staff offices, being most appropriate with its wood panelled rooms. A small flat roofed entrance and security office was made which still stands today - protruding from the southern side of the stable block courtyard.

Before June 1945 an additional building which was used as a mock-up shop had been constructed on the site of the present Belfast Hangar between the main road and the carriage house. A storage building called a Robin hangar was constructed south of the stable block.

The archway into the stables in 1945

The main classroom block and libraries 1945

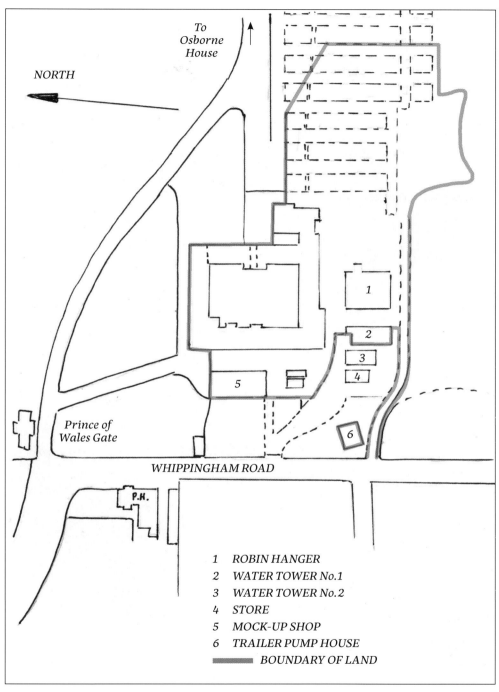

To
Osborne
House

NORTH

1
2
3
4
5
6

Prince of
Wales Gate

WHIPPINGHAM ROAD

P.H.

1   ROBIN HANGER
2   WATER TOWER No.1
3   WATER TOWER No.2
4   STORE
5   MOCK-UP SHOP
6   TRAILER PUMP HOUSE
━━━━━   BOUNDARY OF LAND

Saunders Roe use of the Stable Block and associated land 1945

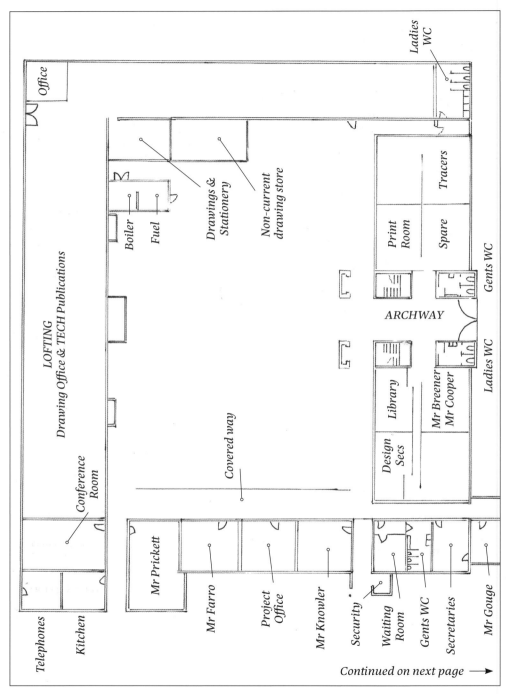

Saunders Roe use of ground floor accommodation from 1945

On 17th December 1945 Saunders Roe received the lease of the whole of the Osborne Stable Block, the Cochrane building and a considerable area of land to the east from Crown Estates.

At this stage Captain Clarke was Managing Director at Saunders Roe with Mr Nelson as Company Secretary. Mr Arthur Gouge had joined Saunders Roe

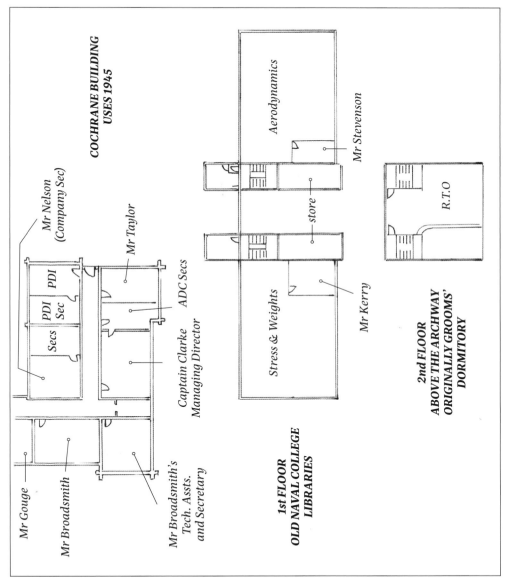

Saunders Roe use of upper floors and Cochrane building from 1945

The small security entrance was added by Saunders Roe

as Chief Executive, with vast design skills, and Mr Broadsmith retired as Chief Designer. They occupied the best offices in the Cochrane Building.

By 1947 the company had built a 618 foot long test tank at the site of the Naval College hospital, opposite Barton Manor lodges, to complete the proving of the designs produced at the Stable block.

By the mid-1950s, a single storey flat roofed structure covered three quarters of the courtyard within the stable block. The roof was supported by a number of vertical pillars, pitched about ten feet apart. Each pillar was about 15 inches in diameter with an internal drainage pipe down the middle. The Design Office took over this large area. Many of those working there were quite oblivious to the fact that they were working in what had been Queen Victoria's stable yard!

In 1959 the complete Design Office comprised the Drawing Office, the Technical Department (known as the Stress and Weights Department,) and the Aerodynamics department. The latter two departments occupied the upstairs college library rooms.

Design engineering was complex, with three main chiefs, who included the Structural Design Chief: Alec Prickett, the mechanical Engineering Chief: Len Summers, and the Electrical Engineering Chief: Dennis Goodings. The aircraft design office was a very busy place in the late fifties and early sixties. Design always began in the Drawing Office, which supported forty draughtsmen

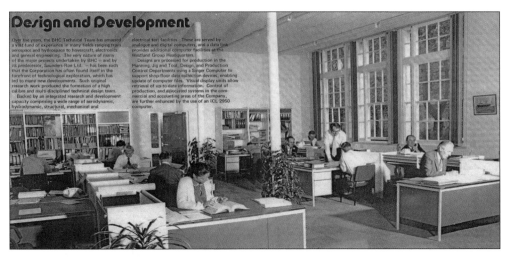

Design and Development

Over the years, the BHC Technical Team has amassed a vast fund of experience in many fields ranging from aerospace and hydrospace to hovercraft, electronics and general engineering. The very nature of many of the major projects undertaken by BHC — and by its predecessor, Saunders-Roe Ltd. — has been such that the Corporation has often found itself in the forefront of technological exploration, which has led to many new developments. Such original research work produced the formation of a high calibre and multi-disciplined technical design team.

Backed by an integrated research and development capacity comprising a wide range of aerodynamic, hydrodynamic, structural, mechanical and electrical test facilities. These are served by analogue and digital computers, and a data link provides additional computer facilities at the Westland Group Headquarters.

Designs are processed for production in the Planning, Jig and Tool, Design, and Production Control Departments using a Singer Computer to support shop-floor data collection devices, enabling update of computer files. Visual display units allow retrieval of up-to-date information. Control of production, and associated systems in the commercial and accounting areas of the Company, are further enhanced by the use of an ICL 2950 computer.

Working in the converted stables

or more, drawing the design details. Any new project needed the recommendation of the Chief Designer, who in 1959 was Richard Stanton Jones.

In 1959 the whole area of the Drawing Office was buzzing with a vast range of technical projects. For instance, one day young Colin Arnold, newly appointed, found himself working opposite a senior draughtsman who was soon complaining about having to draw endless large circles for sections of space rocket drawings that he was preparing. Colin himself was involved in copying rough sketches and trying to convert them into proper technical drawings for parts of an aircraft vehicle drive shaft detail. The Chief Draughtsman, Wally Peters, made an unexpected

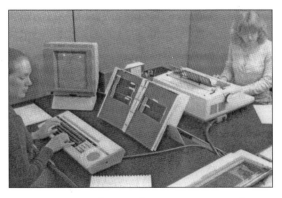

Early word processors were in use

The drawing office in the courtyard

appearance and a whisper went round, *"Keep your heads down!"* He did stop briefly by Colin, and, seeing a new member of staff, checked to see what Colin was doing.

Draughtsmen at work

All designs had to ultimately be approved by the Stress Office, where Colin, as an Apprentice Engineer, was shortly transferred. This office was initially upstairs in one of the old college libraries. Work began daily at 9 o'clock in this office. Colin was amused to learn that one of the annual holidays was in lieu of Queen Victoria's birthday. Another privilege was a free tea-trolley cup of tea in the morning and afternoon, and a free slab of cake during the afternoon tea round. Morning cheese or buttered rolls had to be paid for. Many of the staff took a lunchtime walk along to Queen Victoria's church, St. Mildred's, at Whippingham – a tradition that continues to this day among staff of GKN. Another stroll was down Cadet's Walk towards the river.

The toilets used by the majority of the men were outside the stable block, the old latrine block of the Naval College. A ladies cloakroom had been created in the north-east corner of the stable block itself. New toilets for Senior Staff and Managers were installed in 1945 internally by the Cochrane building. However, if it was raining, we understand that some lesser members of staff broke the "Senior Staff Only" rule and nipped into the managers' conveniences!

While the Government cancelled many projects, often in a late stage of development, it was the development of the hovercraft that kept the company in business for many years. Colin Arnold remembers when a representative of Lloyds of London visited the Stress Office to discuss the licensing of the hovercraft. Colin was working on the SRN5, calculating the overall bending of the structure, using pen, paper and slide rule. Their visitor was surprised at how many detailed calculations were done, as their usual checks with naval architects only involved using established rules of thumb. George Thompson was then given the job of Licensing Officer, and Ray Wheeler acquired the job of Chief Stressman, later becoming Technical Director.

Up to 1959 Saunders Roe were builders of aircraft and marine craft. At this point the company became the Saunders Roe Division of Westland Aircraft Ltd and continued to be builders of marine craft but only aircraft components, not complete aircraft. This is one example of decision making being taken off the Island as local companies are taken over by others with national headquarters off the Island.

The British Hovercraft Corporation logo

The involvement of the National Research and Development Corporation (NRDC) in hovercraft development eventually caused a new company to be formed in 1966 by the amalgamation of three companies involved in hovercraft construction, including Saunders Roe. The new company was called The British Hovercraft Corporation (BHC). This company had its offices at the Stable Block and by 1971 it was a wholly owned subsidiary of Westland Aircraft. The name Saunders Roe disappeared from East Cowes.

A separate building was constructed to the east of the Cochrane building to form a new Stress Workshop, together with the Directors' dining room. This was in the 1970s as part of the Westland Aircraft investment in the offices at the Stable Block.

By 1980 the fluctuations in Westland's sale of hovercraft had caused the production of these vehicles to be uneconomic. In 1985 the company became known as Westland Aerospace Ltd, a subsidiary of the Westland Group of companies. The directors decided to concentrate on high technology components for aircraft, and consolidate their working area. So, in 1982, the Stress Office was moved into the old stable area, closer to the Design Office, in an attempt at an open plan office for a helicopter project.

The Westland Aircraft Ltd. logo

Work continued, but with space in other facilities in East Cowes becoming available, there was no longer any need for the company to occupy the Stable block. In April 1987 Westland Aerospace gave up their lease and moved out of the Osborne Stable Block.

Planes, Hovercraft & Rockets designed at the Stable Block

The SR.A1 jet fighter flying boat.

Early in 1942 the Admiralty decided to request proposals from industry for a fighter aircraft that could take off and land on water. In early 1943 the Chief Designer of the firm of Shorts joined Saunders Roe. He was Arthur Gouge and was appointed Chief Executive and Vice Chairman at East Cowes. His arrival considerably strengthened the long experience of the company in flying boat design and construction.

In July 1943 the SARO design department, under Chief Designer Henry Knowler and Arthur Gouge, produced a design for a jet-propelled flying boat fighter plane. When the war ended, the desire to complete this plane was less urgent. The prototype plane was first launched from the Columbine Shed and flew in July 1947. Known as the *SR.A1*, it was nick-named *"The Squirt"* by the work force. A second craft began trials in 1948 and the third in 1949. It was this aircraft which hit a submerged object while landing off East Cowes and sank, but not before the pilot, Eric Brown, had been rescued by fellow test pilot Geoffrey Tyson, who had been in the company's launch. The plane was never located.

Five weeks later the second prototype crashed off Felixstowe while the pilot, Peter Major, was practising for an aerobatics display. Both plane and pilot were lost. Limited trials continued, but the government decided not to continue with the plane. The remaining *"Squirt"* is on display at Southampton Solent Sky Aero-Museum in 2019.

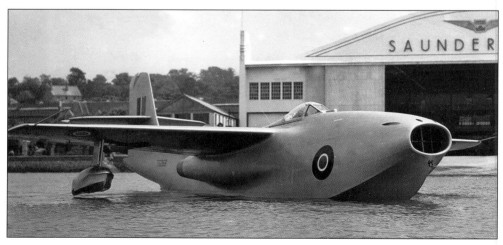

SR.A1 the Squirt

The SR.45 Princess Flying Boat

A study of probable post-war civil aircraft production completed by Saunders Roe in 1943 concluded that there was *"a definite and worthwhile place in post-war aerial transport for the flying boat, particularly for long range work."* On the strength of this report, designs were developed at the Osborne Stable Block for a plane carrying 100 passengers that could cross the Atlantic and be used on other intercontinental routes. Post WWII there was a period of austerity causing restrictions in the use of materials. After many meetings with the Government and British Overseas Airways Corporation, Saunders Roe produced the specifications and design for *SR.45* – the *Princess* flying boat. The company were asked to guarantee that they would fund all capital requirements themselves, and on agreement, the Ministry of Supply gave the Instruction to Proceed with three aircraft in May 1946. The first aircraft left the Columbine works in October 1951 – the largest aeroplane ever to be built in that hangar. The tail and wings had to be completed on the slipway, so that she, registered G-ALUN, was not ready to launch until August 20th 1952. The plane was the largest metal seaplane in the world. It was so large that to get out of the Medina River past the breakwater men had to get out onto the tip of one wing and thus tilt the plane to get the other wing over the breakwater.

SR.45 the Princess Flying Boat

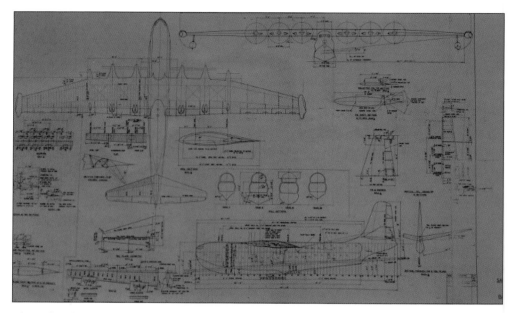

Plans for the SR.45

She started undergoing taxiing trials on August 22nd with Geoffrey Tyson as test pilot, and after only 28 minutes Tyson announced casually to the crew, *"She's unstuck,"* as the plane left the water and was airborne. 35 minutes later they landed after a trip around the Isle of Wight – much to everyone's surprise, and had to do it again for the Press the next day. 90 hours of test flying followed.

Sadly, a few months after the first flight, BOAC announced that the craft were, *"out of date technically."* Additionally, the later stages of the war had resulted in many new concrete runways which were ideal for civil aircraft use, as BOAC had found. Improved engines for the *Princess* would not be available until 1957, and although in 1953 Aquila Airways offered to buy the three planes that had been built, for reasons never declared, the Minister of Supply, Mr Duncan Sandys, refused their offer. The planes were cocooned, first at Medina Road slipway in west Cowes, and then at Calshot until they were sold for scrap in 1965.

The SR.53 Rocket and jet-propelled interceptor fighter plane

The Design Office at the Osborne Stable Block had not been idle since the *SR.A1* jet plane and the *Princess* designs were completed. They had been considering other options including a land-based jet fighter plane. The political situation was causing the Government to consider the need for a rapid response aircraft. In

SR.53 rocket and jet-propelled fighter plane.   Tony Harrison from photograph

1952 they gave Saunders Roe permission to go ahead with their ideas and design a fighter plane that would take off using a rocket engine to climb to 50,000 feet in just over two minutes then use a jet engine to fly at up to Mach 1.8 at 35,000 feet. In 1953 the company was awarded the contract for the design and construction of the *SR.53*.

After the first plane was completed in East Cowes in 1956, the wings were removed so that the plane could be transported in sections to Boscombe Down. The rocket engines used Hydrogen Test Peroxide (HTP) – a very hazardous fuel – but the ground crew gained valuable experience of it with this plane. The first flight was in May 1957, by the company's chief test pilot, John Booth, who completed thirty one successful flights. The second aircraft was completed by Christmas that year, but after eleven successful flights it crashed on take off, killing John Booth.

After extensive investigations with little result, test pilot Peter Lamb continued test flights in the first plane, concluding in his report that *"SR.53 is an extremely docile and exceedingly pleasant aircraft to fly."* However, in 1960 the company was informed by the Ministry of Aviation that the research programme had been abandoned and that no further work was to be carried out on *SR.53*. She is on display at the Aerospace Museum at Cosford in 2019.

The SR.177 fighter plane

Another Government turn-around was responsible for the scrapping of the next project to be designed – the *SR.177*. This fighter plane was designed as a development of the *SR.53* to carry more equipment and to be flexible to keep place with new operational requirements

A mock-up of the SR.177

as they arose. In 1956 the company was given the contract to supply twenty seven of these aircraft.

In 1957, the Minister of Defence, Duncan Sandys, and all his colleagues, stated that all fighter projects should be cancelled and instead defence would be concentrated on ground-to-air guided missiles. By then, the design was 90% complete and the first aircraft was 50% complete. 8,000 drawings had been issued by the Stable Block Design Office and 1,470 staff were made redundant.

The Black Knight, Black Arrow and Falstaff Rockets

The loss of the *SR.177* contract was not a fatal blow to the company as they had been working closely with the Royal Aircraft Establishment (RAE). In March 1955 the guided weapons experts at RAE invited Saunders Roe to design a guided weapons test vehicle. The company's experience in the design and handling of engines using HTP was a major factor in this decision. In June the company was told *"to go full speed ahead"* with developing a rocket-powered vehicle. It was code named *"Black Knight"* and was part of the medium range ballistic missile project, *Blue Streak*. The basic design was drawn up in 1956 at the Stable Block and the first prototype *Black Knight* engine

The Black Knight rocket

mud flats, shallow tidal waters, tundra and ice. Licence agreements were made with companies from Japan to Canada giving the rights to build hovercraft, with design and technical experiences to be shared with Saunders Division of Westlands. Other hovercraft were designed for uses such as transporting heavy loads on roads.

SR.N3

This hovercraft was designed as a military transport vehicle, carrying both men and vehicles. It was the first hovercraft to be produced in any numbers.

The *XS.655* version of these was tested by the Inter-Services Hovercraft Trials Unit for eight years with a view to the Navy using hovercraft for mine counter-measures. Eventually, in 1974, as a test to destruction, its resilience to underwater mines was investigated by setting off a large seabed charge next to the craft in an attempt to turn it over and break its back. Amid a column of water and seabed gravel the craft rose on her five foot cushion of air then settled back on the water. The hovercraft proceeded back to shore under her own power and was scrapped. Further trials were carried out by the Navy using *SR.N4* and *BH.7* versions over several years. All the trials were successful. However in January

SR.N3

1985 the Navy decided not to use hovercraft. The Naval Hovercraft Trials Unit was disbanded and all the work and expense was wasted. Every navy in the world was watching the progress of the testing and waiting for the Admiralty to decide whether to incorporate hovercraft into the counter-measures fleet. As a result of the Navy's decision no orders were received for this type of hovercraft. If hovercraft had been accepted by the Royal Navy, the works at East Cowes may not have been large enough to handle the potential contracts.

SR.N4

This was designed in 1970 to serve on the Cross-Channel service. *Mark 2* could take 37 cars and 282 passengers. In 1978 the *Mark 3*, soon to be known as the *Super 4*, appeared, slowly emerging from the Columbine shed. It had been stretched with the addition of a 55ft-long central section. The Chief Designer, Ray Wheeler, wondered at this point if it could ever hover – but it did. It was the largest hovercraft built by the company and could carry 418 passengers and sixty cars. The two craft, *"Princess Anne"* and *"Princess Margaret"* of this Mountbatten Class continued to serve on the Dover-Calais route for 21 years.

SR.N4 Princess Margaret as the Mark 2 version

SR.N4 Princess Anne as the Mark 3 stretched version

SR.N5

SR.N5 / 6

These were the most successful of the smaller passenger craft, operating world-wide. Locally they went into service on the Ryde – Southsea service, and on the Cowes – Southampton service. There were 55 SR.N6 craft built.

BH.7 military hovercraft

BH.7 Mark 2

This was a hovercraft designed for the Royal Navy. Four *BH.7 Mark 4* craft were built for the Imperial Iranian Navy.

15 other designs were discussed by BHC designers to show that air-cooled diesel engines could be used in hovercraft to save costs. The successful result, the *AP1-88*, carried 80 passengers. The first of these hovercraft was launched at Bembridge in July 1982.

CHAPTER EIGHT

1987 – 2019
More industry in the
Stable Block

National recognition for the Stable Block

In 1987 it was realised that the Stable Block building had some significance in the overall understanding of the Osborne Estate. It was felt that only the arched entrance and original stable wings were worthy of listing as little could be seen of the rest of the structure. These parts of the Stable Block were then listed Grade II as offices. The centre of the courtyard was still covered with temporary buildings, so the remainder of the block was not listed.

The Water Towers and Latrine block were listed Grade II. How many other Grade II Listed toilets are there on the Isle of Wight – or anywhere? Being within the environs of the listed block, the rest of the Stable Bock is now seen as important.

Village Collection 1987 - 1991

After Westland Aircraft left the Osborne Stable Block in 1987, a pine furniture assembly firm called Village Collection took on the lease. The firm of Village Collection were based in Three Gates Road, Cowes, according to their bill head of 1990.

That address may have been a previous letter heading, as by 1990 construction of pine furniture was taking place in the temporary buildings covering the central courtyard of the Stable Block. In March that year the authors purchased a table and chairs direct from the works, followed in June by a cupboard.

Pine chairs and table manufactured at the Stable Block

The impression of the works was of lots of machinery and dust. The furniture was still giving good service in 2019.

After the factory moved out in about 1991, the buildings remained empty for several years and dereliction set in.

English Heritage

English Heritage has a lease on the Osborne Estate from the Crown Estates but this excludes the Stable Block and its surroundings. In 1996 English Heritage approached the government and Crown Estates seeking funding to extend their policy of presenting the Osborne Estate to the public as it was in the 1860s to include the stable block. Their proposal was to remove all evidence of the Royal Naval College Osborne and return the stable block to its appearance in 1861.

The whole building would then be used as an interpretation centre for Osborne. However the budget for this project was very large and it was turned down. English Heritage had already encroached onto unused land next to the Stable Block for their coach park. In 2000 English Heritage commissioned a survey of the whole estate that Victoria and Albert had built up. The document was called The Osborne House Conservation Plan. The consultants expressed concern that there was no conservation plan to protect the fabric of the buildings of the wider estate, most of which remains as Victoria knew it. This includes farms, lodges, cottages and the remains of the Naval College.

The year 1998 brought about another change when Crown Estates granted a lease on the large shed between the stable block and the main road to a business man, Anthony Harrison and his wife. The next stage in the life of the Stable Block was about to begin.

Vectis Storage   1998 onwards

In 1998 Tony Harrison, his wife Marion and his business partner Colin Bedford were operating a storage and removal firm in Lugley Street, Newport. They required more storage facilities and after discussions with the manager of Osborne House they managed to get a rolling six month tenancy from April 1998 on the empty Belfast building between the Osborne Stable Block and the main road. The rest of the stable block was empty and becoming derelict. There was a growing problem with vandalism. Little maintenance was being carried out.

In 1999 Prince Charles visited Osborne to re-open the refurbished Durbar Room. Afterwards he asked to see the Stable Block. He briefly entered the courtyard area, much of which had been enclosed by Saunders Roe for their design office. The view was an area of devastation and decay. Two weeks later, Crown Estates telephoned Marion Harrison and asked if Tony and she would be interested in taking out a 50 year repairing lease on the whole of the site!

Over the previous year, since moving into the Belfast building, Tony had learnt more about the Stable Block site. Where there was once so much life and history, the building was now on the brink of dereliction. After much consideration, and disregarding sensible advice, Mr and Mrs Harrison decided to undertake the huge task of bringing the properties into a good state of repair and took on the lease of the Stable Block on 1st April 2000. It was not a joke!

The firm, Vectis Storage, was formed in the year 2000, and the Harrisons gave up the removals side of the business to concentrate on the storage business, together with the restoration of the Stable Block. Colin Bedford, long-time friend of the Harrisons, became a partner in the storage business and restoration project. His unpaid building skill, knowledge and labour were invaluable. In addition, his financial assistance allowed the project to continue on track.

Tony and Colin started by removing all the "temporary" buildings that filled the courtyard which had been erected by Saunders Roe. The next stage in 2001 was to repair the roof and then the roof-lights in the main classroom block – the old libraries – and the room above the archway. Years of water ingress had severely damaged the parquet flooring, the remainder of which was lifted and dried out carefully. The parquet flooring in the top room over the archway has been lovingly replaced and the rest was stored until a suitable time for replacement occurs.

In 2002 work started on restoring the two water towers and toilet block, and repairs to the Belfast building. The next year, work started on the stable block classroom windows, many of which had to be replaced.

The Cochrane Building – the old classroom block – was in a poor

The infill drawing offices removed from the courtyard

The library roof restored

The restored roof-light above the archway

Parquet floor restored in the top room

state. It had been built specifically for the Naval College, and was not Listed. In 2003 Tony was told that the Cochrane building could be demolished but it had such character that Tony and Colin decided to restore it, thus preserving one of the buildings built specifically for the Naval College. So in 2004 Tony lifted all the roof tiles, replaced rafters where necessary, repaired the cupolas that vented the rooms, and any window frames that were suffering, bringing the building back to excellent condition. *"Old buildings need new uses"* is a catch phrase from English Heritage – storage and office space were provided in the Cochrane building. English Heritage decided that it should be preserved, and it was then Listed Grade II.

Cochrane block under repair

Cochrane block restoration complete

Other rooms around the quadrangle courtyard received similar restoration. On the south side the original tack and harness rooms had been turned into classrooms by the addition of large windows to the south. The slate roof had survived the wartime bombing but, by 2004, needed complete overhaul, which it received.

The rendered external walls needed attention in many places. Lime render was used to match the original. Signs relating to the Naval College have been

South side of the stable block restored

Osborne Stable block Business Park

preserved as they were, and there are still some hitching rings remaining from the Victorian stable.

At one stage Tony hoped to set up a proper display space in the two main classroom blocks, the site of the original stables. This would have shown the numerous uses the Stable Block had experienced. To enable this display, a new purpose built storage shed would need to be constructed and a suitable access to the main road achieved. These criteria were difficult to meet, so a book about the Stable Block was proposed instead.

By 2011 Tony was able to consider some decoration. He produced four very large murals depicting phases of the history of the building. These are on the sloping ceilings of the room above the archway, which Tony refers to as the History Room, once the grooms' dormitory.

In 2014 The Cottage Industry Business Park was established for small businesses needing space to set up in starter units within the Stable Block. Vectis Storage provides the public with individual lock up storage facilities, large or small spaces as required.

For the first time since WWII people began to see the stable block and subsequent Naval College in a new light. Many people had worked for Saunders Roe and British Hovercraft without realising what type of building they were working in.

Tony's dedicated work and enthusiasm for the Stable Block has resulted in interpretation boards being put on display, and even some minor archaeology. 1950s concrete flooring in the courtyard had to be removed to discover the whereabouts of the drainage system installed in 1860. This has now been left visible for the public. He also excavated the remains of one of the white tiled plunge pools that were at the ends of each of the dormitory blocks. Restoration of this pool awaits the time and money as it is lower down on the list of restoration priorities.

The uncovered SE corner of the courtyard

East Cowes now has a much used storage facility and business space. Constant restoration work has been carried out over the ensuing years. Thanks to Vectis Storage the building and heritage of the Stable Block and subsequent Naval College additions within his remit have been saved.

The plunge pool awaiting restoration

The dynamo house from the Naval College is now the responsibility of Scottish and Southern Electricity. It still provides the electricity supply to the Stable Block but is in poor condition and requires restoration.

CHAPTER NINE

The impact of the Stable Block on East Cowes

1860 – 1902 The Stables

In 1859, when the Stable Block was being built for Queen Victoria and Prince Albert, there would have been the opportunity for local builders to gain work in its construction. We know that the Queen was keen to provide labour for local people whenever she could. The Queen's brickyard, near the present Crematorium roundabout on the road out of East Cowes, provided all the red bricks and drainage pipes for Osborne House, the 1861 Stable Block and all the rebuilt estate cottages. A second smaller brickyard on the Queen's estate near Kings Quay produced yellow bricks and both types of these bricks can be seen in the flooring of the stable block.

After completion, the impact of the Stable Block on East Cowes would have been minimal as the Queen's servants travelled with her as she moved around the country. Fodder and straw for the horses would have been provided by Barton Farm, or possibly one of her other six farms in the neighbourhood.

The Forge at Whippingham came within the Queen's estate. This was improved and catered for all the metalwork on the estate and shoeing farm horses. Features of the original forge can still be seen, such as the tethering rings, anvil, bellows and the wheelwright's mandrel. The Forge still thrives in 2019.

When the Queen was in residence there was a much larger stable workforce who needed the services provided in the town – such as cobblers and clothiers. We do not know if all the laundry was done at Osborne, or whether some was passed out to local firms.

Local suppliers were called upon when a full stable staff was in residence at the Stable Block. Roberton's, the main grocers, displayed the "By Appointment"

The forge in 2019

crest above their premises. Slades, one of the East Cowes butchers, was selling surplus meat from the Queen's Barton Manor Farm. We know that fruit and vegetables were sent down from the permanent kitchen gardens at Windsor, but this may just have supplied the main house. The walled garden at Osborne was used mainly for the propagation of trees, bushes and other plants for the grounds, not to supply the kitchen during Victoria's stay.

East Cowes grew rapidly during Victorian times, due to the expansion of local shipbuilding industry and the impact of the royal estate. Any married staff living out would have used the town shops and facilities. The town provided everything that was necessary. Those who retired from the Queen's service sometimes decided East Cowes was the place to live out the rest of their days, such as George Bourner, the Queen's coachman, who lived in Osborne Road and is buried at Kingston Cemetery, East Cowes with his Island-born wife.

Another impact of the Stable Block on the community was the increase in road traffic when the Royal Family were in residence. There would have been more attention paid to the condition of the roads by the East Cowes Council, such as the need to fill in pot holes in the sand and gravel surface and the watering of the roads in summer to keep the dust down. The old maps of the town show a number of gravel pits by the main roads.

1903 – 1921 College impact and visible remains

Local labour was required to help in the construction of the Naval College. This took place over two years, with further additions as time went on. We know that the East Cowes firm of W.H.Brading was involved in the alterations to the stable block and work involved with the engineering workshops. At the start of WWI additional buildings were required for the increased number of Cadets recruited. The size of the town grew as teaching staff chose to have houses built in the town by local builders, such as W.H.Brading, who had their own quay and workshops by the river.

The arrival of the boys at the Naval College was a different matter. Hundreds of boys and staff needed a lot of provisions. Food and milk were obtained locally, delivered to the kitchens daily. The local farmers and shops must have benefited considerably. We know that the contract to repair all of the Cadets' shoes and boots was given to Turner's shoe shop in Ferry Road. The increased population would have encouraged the local shopkeepers.

Quite a few of the Petty Officers were married, and, with their wives and families, settled in East Cowes. Two of them were Chief Petty Officer Robert Aitken who served at the college during WWI, but Stoker William Cake was not so lucky. He had been working at the Naval College but was sent back to sea in 1914 and died when *HMS Hood* was sunk. Cake left a wife and seven children in East Cowes. Both Aitken and Cake families still live in the town. Younger men stationed at the College sometimes met East Cowes girls and married here. Mr Boissier, the history master, married the daughter of the vicar of Whippingham.

The Naval College sent seamen, Marines and Petty Officers from the College to help douse a fire at International Stores in 1905, preventing the fire spreading to neighbouring properties. They brought the College manual fire pump with them. After this fire, the Town Council decided to create an East Cowes fire brigade and bought their own steam water pump. The Naval staff from the college and training vessels also helped extinguish several other major fires in the town, such as at J S White's shipyard at Cowes in 1911.

Turner Brothers boot and shoe repair shop in Ferry Road, after 1908

The East Cowes laundry flourished in Victoria Road (the name changed to Kings Road in 1934). The laundry for all the boys had to be washed by someone. Sheets were hung to dry on the fields of Kingston Farm, still Crown Estate, so presumably a drying ground was established there. More jobs were created in the town associated with the college.

The staff took part in events and entertainments at East Cowes Town Hall. One event was a marathon piano playing session, by Marine Private George Doughty from the Naval College.

Local photographers and printers were used by the college. Many term photographs of the boys and the sports team photographs were taken by the photographer William Kirk. Kirk also covered Royal visits to the college. Many postcards of life at the Naval College and the premises were printed and sold to the cadets to send home to their families.

The boys themselves were not allowed to go off the campus, unless taken out by relatives on a Sunday afternoon. That would give the teashops in the town an opportunity to sell copious numbers of buns! The onsite tuck shop was popular.

Two streets in the town recall the Naval College, namely College Way and Cadets' Walk. Cadets' Walk was the path used almost daily by the boys to go

Mr and Mrs Boissier at Whippingham Rectory

Marathon piano playing

Remains of the Cadet's walkway

The organ in situ at ORNC and now at Adelaide Grove Methodist Church

to the Naval College Engineering Workshops by the river. These included two boys who were later to become King Edward VIII and King George VI. This path was edged with heavy black engineering-quality bricks. King Edward VII and his son (later King George V) walked up Cadets' Walk to the Stable Block after the King had opened the Engineering Works in 1903.

When the college closed, the organ from the balcony in the Nelson Building went to the Methodist Church in Adelaide Grove, East Cowes, where it can still be seen and heard.

The departure of the Naval Cadets and staff dramatically reduced the custom for East Cowes shops and businesses. Local farmers had to seek new outlets.

Prince Edward started at ORNC in 1907

1921 – 1939 Alternative Uses

During the occupation of the college by the Voluntary Aid Detachment nurses for the summer camps at the end of the 1920s local suppliers benefited briefly. Mr Tillett of Barton Manor loaned his carts and horses to the VADs during their training. The food for the hundreds of nurses was obtained as locally as possible, and local staff were employed to help cook it in the kitchen at the Stable Block.

The holiday camp established on the College Hospital site opposite Barton Manor gates in the 1930s provided seasonal work for the town - cooking, cleaning and laundry, and the opportunity for market gardeners to cash in. One of these was Mr Othen who had land just south of the holiday camp. He received the food-waste from the holiday camp, which his pigs appreciated. In return he supplied vegetables. Dairy farmers also profited, if they could supply the extra milk required by the camp.

Demolition of many of the temporary college buildings in 1936 provided some work for local men, and anecdotal evidence has mentioned various uses being found for some of the college timber in local homes. Until 1940 East Cowes people did have the use of the Osborne Hall, the old carriage house, as the old dining hall was known, and many lively dances were held there before it was requisitioned.

Barton Manor Farm carts being used for VAD exercises

1939 to the present day - Industry takes over

Indirectly, the training of so many Naval Cadets at the Stable Block helped East Cowes and Britain to survive WWII. Those lads were Captains and senior naval officers by 1939. Many Navy ships that fought in WWII were manned by Officers trained at the Osborne Naval College.

The RAMC created a hospital and had hundreds of personnel stationed at Osborne Stable Block. All needed feeding. Jobs were strictly apportioned in wartime, and food production was controlled, so the people of East Cowes may have been little better off with the influx of medics, although in their spare time the RAMC would have frequented the town, especially the pubs!

Saunders Roe took over some of the site, such as the Osborne Hall, during the war. After the war they took over the whole site, which then provided work, not only for local people, but also attracted a highly skilled additional workforce, many expert in design and electronics. These families moved into the town to work in the expanding aircraft industry. Many new houses were built, not just those to replace the bombed properties. Kent Avenue estate was built specifically for the incoming skilled workforce needed for the production of planes such as

Kent Avenue was built for Saunders Roe technical staff

the *Princess* Flying Boat, launched in 1952. The slogan *"A House with the Job"* was coined to attract the best staff possible. Permission to build was given on the proviso that one of the 120 houses was given to the Council, and all the rest were for Saunders Roe personnel. The Radio Engineer on board the *Princess*, Maurice Mabey, was still living in his same Kent Avenue house at the time of writing. The shops in the town flourished with the increased population.

One important aspect of the management of the shipbuilding and aircraft construction companies in East Cowes was the high quality of the apprenticeships provided for youngsters. The diversification of Saunders Roe from a flying boat construction company into manufacturers of a wide variety of products required all aspects of engineering. This meant that the apprentices working on designs emanating from the drawing office in the Stable Block received as wide an engineering training as possible. This must have been very attractive for youngsters from all areas, not just East Cowes.

The Saunders Roe Apprentice School set up at the College hospital site in 1945 provided employment for local people in catering and teaching. This apprentices' school had a major effect on the training standards achieved for the local aircraft industry, some of the lads later going on to university funded by the company

Saunders Roe apprentices training in a converted ORNC hospital ward

before returning to become designers at the Stable Block and one at least, Ray Wheeler, a director of the company. Engineering training has always been seen as important and continues to this day, now in a new purpose built training centre, the Centre of Excellence for Composites, Advanced Manufacturing and Marine, (CECAMM) built adjacent to GKN, on Mr Othen's old market garden.

Westland Aerospace left the Stable Block in 1987, but the legacy of the design office continues. One effect seen in East Cowes has been the naming of several roads after Saunders Roe Designers who worked at the Stable Block, or their outstanding designs. Hence we have Broadsmith Avenue, named for Harold Broadsmith who was responsible for Technical Design from 1939 to 1945, and Nelson Close was named after Mr Nelson who was Company Secretary. Princess Close was named for the *Princess* Flying Boat, and Black Knight Close, named for the *Black Knight* Rocket, so successful between 1959 and 1965. Then there is Cockerell Rise, named for the inventor of the hovercraft, who stayed at a house on that location in Victoria Grove while liaising with Saunders Roe designers prior to the launch of the first hovercraft in 1959.

Since the arrival of Vectis Storage at the Stable Block, a welcome facility has been provided for local Islanders. Many people need short or long term

A modern training centre for island youth, CECAMM

storage. The Stable Block provides a large quantity of this for individuals and for companies. The business has expanded to provide office space giving different employment possibilities, with several small firms starting up at the Stable Block, or expanding into larger spaces there. The transport companies DHL and Vectis Oils have offices and storage facilities, providing more employment. The Stable Block has gone full circle from Royal horse transport to Islandwide lorry deliveries.

Summary

The Stable Block has proved to be a catalyst for many activities during its complex history. It has seen changes to its structure since first built as a stable and coach house. It was extended upwards for the naval cadets and given new windows for classrooms. The coach house suffered bomb damage but was temporarily re-roofed. Most of the courtyard was covered with concrete and temporary buildings for the Saunders Roe design office. With the clearance of the temporary buildings the courtyard and general structure of the Stable Block can now be seen again as an entity.

Some indicators of the Stable Block history remain, such as the courtyard tiled floor, stable fittings and direction signs for the cadets. Many buildings associated with activities in the Stable Block remain. These include the college water towers, a dormitory plunge pool, the foundations of the officers' accommodation, the Petty Officers accommodation and the Cochrane classrooms. Later history is indicated by the Saunders Roe stress building and the security entrance to the courtyard.

Had the stable block not been built in 1861 by Prince Albert, it could not have been made available after Queen Victoria's death for the core of the Naval College. But it was there, and because of the Naval College the construction of a vast range of additional buildings happened, both adjacent to the stable block and on other sites in the neighbourhood. So the stable block had a snowball effect, allowing many subsequent activities, from a site by the river for an electricity power station and boat building sheds for Uffa Fox, to a site for a holiday camp and engineering apprentices' school, and now a work place for GKN.

It is true that an old building may need a new use to survive. When Prince Albert planned the Stable Block he could never have envisaged the subsequent uses to which the building would be put. Prince Albert embraced modern technology. We like to think that he would have been proud of the excellent training given to the Naval Cadets in nautical subjects in the old stable block. Equally he would have had enthusiasm for the aeroplane, rocket and hovercraft designs that emerged from the design office. Prince Albert would also have been pleased with the restoration work that has been achieved a hundred and fifty years later to reveal the Osborne Stable Block as converted to a Naval College.

The remaining foundations of the Officers' Quarters, ORNC

The seamens' sick bay, now a toilet block in 2019

Today the Stable Block is a hive of activity but passers-by may not see the Stable Block behind the industrial building. Those visiting the house will see the archway entrance to the stables in the distance as they leave. We hope that this book will encourage people to understand the true value and impact of the Osborne Stable Block.

The 1861 stable block in use as business premises in 2019

Acknowledgements

The authors would like to thank the following people for their help in finding and confirming information used in this book.

Mr Tony Harrison, leaseholder of the Osborne House Stable Block.
Michael Hunter, Curator of Osborne House.
Richard Smout, County Archivist, Isle of Wight County Records Office.
Corina Westwood, Isle of Wight Heritage Service.
Alice Walsh, Royal Naval Library, Portsmouth.
The Museum Staff at the Royal Naval College Britannia, Dartmouth
Michael Partridge, author of *The Royal Naval College Osborne – A History 1903-21.*
Geoffrey Haskins, author of *The School that Jack Built – The Royal Naval College Osborne 1903 – 1921.*
The staff at The National Archives, Kew.
Mr and Mrs de Courcy-Ireland for information about George Bourner, one of Queen Victoria's coachmen.
Colin Arnold for his memories of working in the drawing office of Saunders Roe.

Ken Wheeler of Pressready Artwork for his suggestions, patience and hard work in preparing the material for publication.

Index

Colin Bedford

Marion Harrison

Tony Harrison and his team renovating the Osborne Stable Block in 2008.